AS and A2 Media Studies: The Essential Revision Guide

AS and A2 Media Studies: The Essential Revision Guide hensively updated new edition offering advice and guidance to help students pass AS and A2 Media Studies.

Written by a team of experienced teachers and examiners, the book offers clear and engaging pathways through all the areas covered in the Media Studies curriculum, providing students with:

- revision activities
- exam tips and reminders
- definitions of key terms
- past paper questions
- references to examiners' reports.

The authors also offer essential background information to help Media Studies students understand wider contexts and theoretical perspectives, as well as giving the lowdown on how exams are marked, how to manage self-study and approaching final examinations.

Antony Bateman has taught Media and Film Studies for fourteen years and was formerly Diploma Programme Director for Creative and Media in Rochdale. He is co-author of *A2 Media Studies: The Essential Introduction for AQA* (second edition, 2010), *AS Media Studies: The Essential Introduction for WJEC* (2011) and *A2 Media Studies: The Essential Introduction for WJEC* (2010).

Sarah Casey Benyahia is a Media and Film Studies teacher at Colchester Sixth Form College. She is a senior examiner for one of the major assessment boards and the co-author of several textbooks, including *A2 Media Studies: The Essential Introduction for AQA* (second edition, 2010), *AS Media Studies: The Essential Introduction for WJEC* (2011) and *A2 Media Studies: The Essential Introduction for WJEC* (2010) and *AS and A2 Film Studies: The Essential Introduction* (2009).

Claire Mortimer has been involved in teaching Media and Film Studies for over 20 years. She has had extensive experience as an Assistant Examiner for Media Studies. She is the author of the *Routledge Film Guidebook: Romantic Comedy* (2010), and co-author of *AS Media Studies: The Essential Introduction for WJEC* (2011) and *Doing Film* (2012).

Peter Wall has over 40 years of experience of teaching in further and higher education and providing support for schools and colleges. He has held a number of senior examining positions for awarding bodies and currently acts as Chair of Examiners for GCE and GCSE Media Studies for a major awarding body. He is the author of several textbooks for Media Studies and related disciplines in addition to his role as series editor for Routledge Essentials.

AS and A2 Media Studies: The Essential Revision Guide for AQA

Second edition

ANTONY BATEMAN, SARAH CASEY BENYAHIA, CLAIRE MORTIMER AND PETER WALL

Routledge
Taylor & Francis Group

LONDON AND NEW YORK

First published 2014
by Routledge
2 Park Square, Milton Park, Abingdon, Oxon OX14 4RN

Simultaneously published in the USA and Canada
by Routledge
711 Third Avenue, New York, NY 10017

Routledge is an imprint of the Taylor & Francis Group, an informa business

British Library Cataloguing in Publication Data
A catalogue record for this book is available from the British Library

ISBN: 978-0-415-53411-6 (hbk)
ISBN: 978-0-415-53393-5 (pbk)
ISBN: 978-0-203-11373-8 (ebk)

Typeset in Charter
by Keystroke, Station Road, Codsall, Wolverhampton

Printed and bound in Great Britain by
TJ International Ltd, Padstow, Cornwall

Contents

Illustrations

Acknowledgements

We acknowledge the AQA exam board for their permission to reproduce examination questions in this book.

PART I

INTRODUCTION

GETTING STARTED

Thank you for buying our book. We very much hope that you will find it a useful aid to your preparation for your GCE Media Studies exams.

This book is divided into two sections: the first deals with how best to revise and prepare for your AQA GCE Media Studies AS exam known as MEST 1, Investigating Media; the second part of the book is focused on the AQA GCE Media Studies A2 examination, Media: Critical Perspectives. Before you start using the book, you need to make sure that:

- you are in fact preparing for the AQA qualification. Check with your teacher that AQA is the awarding body whose exams you will be taking.
- you know which part of the course you are taking. AS exams are usually sat during your first year of study and A2 exams during your second year. One possible exception to this is if you are retaking your AS exam, which you will most likely do in the second year.

> **NOTE**
>
> The term GCE, short for General Certificate of Education, is interchangeable for most students with the term 'A' Levels. However, the term is used by AQA to avoid confusion now that the GCE qualification has been split into AS and A2 Levels.

This book has been written specifically to help you prepare for this AQA qualification. If you are preparing to sit another awarding body's exams, you will probably do better to find a revision book specifically designed to help you with that qualification.

This is a good point to ask yourself just why you think you need a revision book. Perhaps a more appropriate question might be: What do I hope to get out of this revision book? One thing a revision book is not intended to do is to save you the trouble of revising. Nor can you expect it to rescue you if you have spent much of your course not properly focused on the work you need to have done to be ready for your exam.

This book is designed to help you get the best grade that you are capable of. It will try to do this by suggesting to you the best way to get ready for the exams you need to sit for the two parts of your GCE.

Ideally you will have spent time on your Media Studies course learning some basic and not so basic ideas about what underpins a study of the media. With any luck you will have grown used to using a variety of different tools to help you with your study. These are likely to include:

- close study of media products and the way in which they are constructed
- some of the major issues and debates that inform an intelligent study of the media
- an introduction to some of the key theoretical perspectives that can be used to help us reach a fuller understanding of the role and significance of the media in our lives.

One special skill you should have developed is that of being able to think on your feet, especially when you are confronted with media products that you are not familiar with but which you need to assimilate quickly. You will find some useful tips in this book to help you develop this skill but it is worth keeping in mind how important this ability will be at both AS and A2 levels. Spending a few minutes every day getting used to focusing deeply on a media product or a media issue you happen to come across will significantly enhance your abilities to tackle both the MEST1 and MEST3 exams. Do bear this in mind. There are a number of tips throughout this book which should help you do it.

So how best to use this book? Realise straightaway that when it comes to preparing for exams, there are as many approaches as there are students taking exams. What makes GCE Media Studies different is the fact that it is almost impossible to get away from the subject you are studying. Like it or not, we live in a media-saturated universe. That means that you will be in almost constant contact with the very materials that you need to help you prepare for your exam. Try to use this fact to make sure that you have developed a real sense of what is happening in the world of the media in readiness for the exam.

The AQA specification at both AS and A2 levels places a heavy emphasis on contemporary media output. Examiners who mark your exam script will inevitably be impressed if you can demonstrate an informed awareness of contemporary media output and the issues and debates occasioned by what the media are saying and doing.

The trick then is to use the guidance and advice we offer in this book to help you put this knowledge and awareness of contemporary media activity into an appropriate context to help prepare you for your exam. To get the best from this book, we suggest you read it selectively rather than simply working through it page by page. Use the contents page to identify a particular aspect of the specification that you are revising in preparation for your exam, read it carefully and then think how you can best apply it to your own specific interests. That way you will get the best from the book and at the same time develop your own autonomy in relation to your study of the media. This ability to show that you are able to respond both intelligently and independently to media products and the issues they raise is essential to ensure your success in your exam.

GETTING THE BEST FROM THIS BOOK

So you have decided to read a book on revising for your GCE Media Studies exams. Good. Before you go any further, it is a good idea to think why you have chosen to read this book.

There are a number of possible reasons and knowing which one is most appropriate to you may well help you get the best from this book. The worst-case scenario is that you are going into the exam room in the near future with absolutely no idea of how to tackle the exam or exams you are taking. In this situation you need to read this book fast, try to act on some of the key advice we offer and hope that it is your lucky day when you come to sit down in the exam room. If this really is the case, then, despite the fact that you do not have time to play with, it might be a good idea to work out how you arrived in this mess. It may not be entirely your fault. In the end, however, you do have to take responsibility for your own life and your own future, so, by addressing the issue, it may well be you can find a way forward to ensure that you are better prepared next time.

Another reason you might be reading this book is that you are the type of student who wants to get every bit of help that you possibly can. It may be that you feel by reading this book, you will be getting some extra advice, a little bit of inside information that will give you a good chance of getting really good grades. If this describes you, then certainly the book can help you, particularly in terms of our suggestions for revision, preparation and exam techniques. Don't, however, see the book as an end in itself. There is a real danger with books of this type that students believe the book will do the work for them. This is most certainly not the case. Don't see this as some cynical crib sheet that will get you through your exam. A good media student should be setting their own agenda, not relying on a textbook to do it for them.

Remember that as a student you are an individual with different interests, aptitudes and talents. It follows that you will feel more confident about some areas of the specification (the current jargon for course syllabus) than others. You may feel that you have got a lot out of your Media Studies course, but that you need a little bit of help putting it all together in a way that makes sense when you go into the exam room.

Features of the revision guide

This guide is written with the conscientious and engaged student in mind, but one who may also need some guidance and a few prompts along the way. In each section you will find that we include:

- revision activities
- exam tips and reminders

- definitions of key terms
- past paper questions
- references to examiners' reports.

To get the most from this guide it's important to interact with it – to think about the questions posed, to do the activities set – rather than just to read it and hope that some of the advice will stick.

You can start by writing down the dates and names of the exams you are due to sit and then doing a simple calculation that tells you how long you have to get ready.

The next thing to do is to make some kind of realistic assessment of what you feel confident about and what you don't. It's likely that you will have taken a mock exam of some sort in preparing for your AS Media Studies. This is a good starting point from which to decide where you might need some extra help. It may be that you need to talk to your teacher about your mock to get some advice from him or her about what you need to focus on.

LEARNING FROM YOUR MOCK

Taking a mock exam may not be your favourite pastime, but there is a lot you can learn from the outcome. On p. 17 we suggest that you undertake a SWOT analysis in order to assess your strengths and weakness. A mock exam is a potentially really useful focal point for this activity.

Your teacher will probably have set you questions from a past paper and marked them using the awarding body's mark scheme. This should give you a realistic estimate of how well you might perform in the exam itself. More usefully, however, it should also show you where you have performed well and where you have performed badly.

You should not only make a careful note of the actual marks you have obtained but also check out any ticks or comments your teacher has written on your mock exam script. If necessary, see if your teacher will spend time going through the paper with you and helping you identify your good and bad points.

From this, you should be able to identify those areas that particularly need attention. For example, in your MEST1 mock, you may have answered the short questions in response to the unseen product in Section A especially well and done badly in Section B where you had to write about your cross-media study. Of course this doesn't mean you can forget revising for Section A in the exam proper, but it should suggest that you look closely at what you need to do for the cross-media study question.

Once you have got some sense of what you need, look carefully to see how the book might help you. We have split it into sections so it should be fairly easy to find what you want quickly. The stuff about the exams is mostly in Parts 2 and 3, under the headings of the two AQA exams for which you are preparing: 'Investigating Media', aka MEST1, and 'Critical Perspectives', aka MEST3. This is where you will find direct and detailed advice about how to take a good shot at doing well in the AS and A2 exam.

There is, however, some other useful advice throughout the book and, assuming you have time, then it is a good idea to read it. The section 'What kind of student are you?' (p. 10) provides the key to success or failure in Media Studies exams. It is all about your own independence and confidence in making critical judgements and applying these to media products. If you can get your head around this idea and have the confidence to apply it, you are likely to improve your potential grade quite significantly.

We have also included some suggestions about how to revise. You might find some of this is second nature to you. If so, great – skip it. If not, then open your eyes to how you can do yourself a favour simply by getting yourself organised and ready to take the exams. Remember this is your future, not someone else's. We will spare you the clichés about life not being a dress rehearsal.

NOTE

It is our belief that many students simply do not understand what they are being confronted with when they sit down to take an exam. Increasingly exam awarding bodies and their regulating body, the Office of Qualifications and Examinations Regulation, OFQUAL, talk about transparency and accountability in the exam system. This means that, far from being a system that prevents candidates from knowing how they are assessed, they are encouraged to understand fully the assessment process. You can log on to the websites of AQA and OFQUAL and get a lot of information about the process. The AQA website has become much more student-friendly. It is worth paying it a visit, not least for some of the tips and hints it offers students to help prepare for and take exams. It also gives you access to the specification itself and past papers and mark schemes. Unfortunately AQA are not so enlightened as to publish future papers to help you prepare!

WHY DO WE NEED EXAMS?

During your time in the education system, you will have come across a wide range of different types of examination. Indeed one criticism of education policy is that far too much assessment takes place and that the system has become obsessed with constantly testing young people rather than giving them the opportunity to learn. Whatever the truth of the matter, examinations are here to stay, at least in the short term. One reason that there are so many different sorts of examinations is that each subject or area of the curriculum requires a different approach to testing what you have learned. Some examinations will rely heavily on your ability to learn facts and repeat these in the examination. Other exams will be more concerned with your ability and skills in the application of what you have learned. Media Studies examinations are on the side of the spectrum that concerns itself with the application of skills as opposed to the writing down of learned material. This quality of Media Studies examinations will have important implications for the way in which you approach both the exam itself and your preparation for it.

Before we talk in more detail about the nature of Media Studies exams, it is worth considering what the defining characteristics of examinations are in general. These can range from tests over a period of several hours undertaken over periods of several weeks, common in art and design subjects, to short tests of an hour. So what qualities define such diverse approaches as exams? Well, here are some things they have in common:

- *Externally set*. This means that the question or task that you are asked to complete has been set by the examination board rather than by your school or teacher. What you are asked to do will also be asked of all other candidates throughout the country, and in some cases the world, taking the same paper.
- *Externally assessed*. This means that when you have completed the exam your work is sent off to an examiner whose job it is to mark it along with the exam scripts of several hundred other candidates who have taken the exam. Where you undertake a piece of coursework, this is marked in your centre, usually by your teacher, and then the accuracy and fairness of the marking is checked externally by looking at a small sample of the work from your centre. This process is called internal assessment and the checking is called moderation.
- *Unseen*. Although there are some exceptions, exams are generally unseen, which means that you don't know what is on the exam paper until you open it in the exam room. As you will see later in the book, this does not mean you have no idea what you will be asked and using what you do know is an important factor in getting the odds of success in your favour.
- *Time-constrained*. You have a limited period of time in which to answer the paper. This time limit can vary widely but for most Media Studies exams is in the region of one to two hours. Again time constraint is an important consideration in your exam performance and one we will look at in detail later in the book.

It is important to remember that the chief function of exams is to differentiate levels of achievement. Put more simply, that means to find out the difference between students who have a really good grasp of the subject and those with rather less of a grasp. It is inevitable, therefore, that some candidates will do better than others. Our aim in this book is to help you make sure that you are one of those who do well.

> **NOTE**
>
> Bear in mind that exams are the same for everyone. It is not just you who is under pressure; everyone feels the same. This may appear some small consolation but one important difference is that, while some people let pressure get to them and destroy their chances of doing well, smart people use the pressure to help them. Try to learn to do this. A certain amount of tension and anxiety can actually help you feel sharp and alert when you go into the exam room. Try to create for yourself a frame of mind where you use the energy to focus on the task in hand. A lot of the battle is just about thinking positively and seeing exams as an opportunity rather than a threat.

So, having considered the nature of exams, let's return to our initial question: Why do we need exams? Exams provide an external and objective assessment of the extent and depth of your learning within an area of study. Internal assessment or coursework provides a similar check but is considered by the awarding bodies to be less rigorous than externally assessed forms of testing not least because it is potentially easier for candidates to cheat in their coursework despite the many safeguards that seek to prevent this.

All of this has important implications for how you approach taking exams. On the one hand, you can see exams as something greatly to be feared, some monstrous mechanism for catching you out and exposing your deficiencies or, on the other hand, you can see them as a chance to demonstrate or even show off the skills and knowledge you have developed as part of your study of the media. Needless to say the latter approach is the one we would recommend as the road to success. Indeed one quality of Media Studies examinations is that they invite you to adopt this approach. Their intention is not to catch you out but rather to present you with an opportunity. If you approach your media exams in this way, then you are likely to do well. In this book we tell you some of ways in which you can prepare yourself to take advantage of the opportunity that the exams offer. What we can't do is take the exams for you. If you are to do well, then the hard work is up to you. At least with Media Studies most of this hard work is in some way enjoyable work.

PART 2

AS LEVEL

PREPARING FOR THE AS EXAM

What kind of student are you?

Let us start with a fundamental question: What kind of student are you? Perhaps it would be more precise to ask what kind of Media Studies student you are, because the same student can behave very differently in classes for one subject than for another. In Media Studies there are basically two different types of student:

- passive students
- active students.

Of course, these categories are not watertight and an individual student may well move between the two categories according to many factors, including the topic being studied and their own personal and emotional state. But it is worth considering these two categories to help you focus on how to get the best from your course.

The passive student

The passive student believes that the job of their teacher is to do all the work. For the passive student, turning up at every class, writing down notes and handing in homework is all that is necessary in order to get a good grade in the exam. Passive students want to be spoon-fed information that they can repeat in the exam and pick up a certificate at the end of the course. Passive students usually manage to pass exams, but rarely achieve the grade that they are capable of obtaining. This is especially true if they have a teacher who is happy to do a lot of the work for them by not only choosing the media products and issues they should look at but teaching them how they should respond to them. The reason for this is that the passive student becomes far too heavily reliant on the teacher and never takes the opportunity to engage properly with the discipline of Media Studies or, perhaps more importantly, with the impact that the media has on our lives. Passive students believe that the teacher knows everything they need to know in order to do well in the exam. So long as they listen and do what they are told, the teacher will provide them with the recipe for success.

The active student

Active students want to know. Active students think for themselves. Active students are fun to teach. So what is an active student?

Active students do not rely on the teacher to tell them everything they need to know to pass the exam. Active students know how to get the best from their teacher. Like passive students they listen carefully to what the teacher has to tell them and then they go and test out the ideas for themselves. Part of the pleasure of being a Media Studies student is that many of the products and ideas that you engage with are not only accessible, they are also enjoyable. So if you are an active student and you have been learning about a concept such as genre, you will want to go home and watch some television or go out to the cinema in order to test out the new concept you have learned.

If you are a really active student, you will jot down some ideas about how what you have seen links into the concept of genre as you have had it explained to you by the teacher. If you are a truly hyperactive student, you will want to introduce your ideas about it into the next class you have on genre.

Active students are autonomous. They see Media Studies as a string of concepts or theories that can be applied to a whole range of media products. The autonomy bit comes in when you go out and find what you want to explore through these concepts or theories rather than waiting for your teacher to tell you what you need to look at.

Applying what you know

It is probably quite obvious to you which sort of student we think is likely to do better in Media Studies exams. Rather less obvious perhaps is the reason why this is the case. So let's try to explain.

Media Studies is about concepts rather than knowledge. What that means is that Media Studies examiners are more interested in how you can apply what you know than in simply finding out what you know. For example, you may know about semiotics, you may be able to explain some of the different theories of narrative and you may have a good sense of what is meant by the ideological function of media output. Your Media Studies exam will not, however, ask you what you know about these things, at least not directly. For example, you won't get a question that says: 'What did Roland Barthes consider to be the significance to narrative of the hermeneutic or enigma code?' Such a question would be considered not only completely unfair but quite contrary to the ethos established for examining Media Studies. Much more likely is a question in Section A that asks you about the

function of narrative in the unseen product – it is up to you to decide which aspect of narrative is the most important and relevant. In some ways these questions amount to something very similar except that the first is asking you to write specifically about narrative theory, the second is inviting you to use and apply narrative theory in a useful way to the kind of media that you may well consume on a daily basis.

Both types of question assume that you know about theories of narrative; the second question, however, is asking you to show how narrative theory can be applied to specific media products. So what the latter question is in fact doing is inviting you to demonstrate that you can apply this perspective to specific products you have consumed. This is where being an active student comes into play. An active student, you will remember, is one who will have absorbed the theoretical concept in class, seen the teacher apply it to a range of examples and then gone out to find products of their own – which might become part of your cross-media study – to test out the concept. So, for example, the teacher will have explained how narrative uses enigmas to tease the audience in order to hook them into the narrative flow and ensure that they remain glued to the product until the outcome is revealed.

The teacher may have used examples from crime fiction programmes to exemplify this idea. An episode of *Sherlock*, for example, offers a whole range of enigmas from solving crimes to personal relationships in each episode. At this point the passive student will decide that they have done enough and if they are asked to answer a question on narrative enigmas in the exam, then crime fiction as exemplified will do the job. The active student, however, will realise that crime fiction is a fairly obvious application for this particular concept and will set out to see how well the enigma theory will work with other media output. Soap operas, sitcoms and horror movies might be three alternative areas ripe for exploration with this new tool. So the active student will explore them in a number of ways: first and most obviously by looking at examples typical of these genres. If you think about it, this is a really easy thing to do, given a listings magazine and, if necessary, a look at IMDb.

www.imdb.com/

The next thing that may be useful to do is to engage in some further reading on narrative theory. With luck the teacher might have given some suggestions for this further reading. If not, then any introductory textbook to media theory is likely to have a chapter on narrative theory. A quick scan of the index should also tell you if there is information about enigma codes, too. How much further reading you do is up to you. Certainly your textbook will suggest some possible further reading and you may even consider a quick search of the Web to see if there is anything immediately available.

What is described here constitutes active independent research. It is the approach that good Media Studies students are likely to adopt. So what is good about it? Well, instead of relying on everything that the teacher has told them, these students have taken the idea and tried to find their own application for it. They have tested the idea against products that they have chosen for themselves. They have looked into further reading, both to gain further clarification of the theory and to see what other theorists have made of it. This kind of approach is not only vital to the construction of a successful cross-media study but also to prepare you for the unseen analysis in Section A – the wider experience you have of media products, the more comfortable you will feel with whatever it is you have to analyse in that part of the exam.

There has been a good deal of research into how people learn. One study carried out in the 1970s at the California Institute of Technology looked at how much information people had retained 48 hours after obtaining it through a range of different methods. Their results are interesting:

* lecture 5%
* reading 10%
* audio-visual 20%
* demonstration 30%
* discussion group 50
* practise by doing 75%
* teaching others 90%

NOTE

If you apply these percentages to your own learning, then you are likely to take in about 5% of what your teacher tells you. If you find out for yourself, then this rises dramatically to 75%. If you then come back and tell other people – for example, by giving a presentation to the class – you should be able to retain almost all the information.

Of course, this may not be a wholly accurate representation of how people learn and retain information, but it does a great deal to support the argument that your own independent learning is potentially the most efficient way to prepare yourself for an exam. Relying solely on your teacher is probably the least efficient.

So how will this help in the exam? The answer is in a number of ways:

* Active students will go into the exam room with a personal and, it is to be hoped, memorable experience of this particular element of theory. This means that they are more likely to remember the ideas and the exemplification than if they had simply copied down what they had been told by the teacher. See above.

- The examples which they have chosen will be fresh and distinct from those used by other candidates. When the examiner marks a pile of scripts, s/he is more likely to seek to reward the individual response than the mass-produced responses contained in all the essays containing ideas copied from the teacher.
- Students who have done their own research will be much better equipped to adapt their responses to the actual demands of the question than will students who have a prepared answer based on their teacher's notes. This is very important in the use of your cross-media study in Section B.
- The response of active students will be more accurate than that of passive students. Writing down ideas that you have got second-hand from other people is always a fraught business. It is most unlikely that you will ever do so without at least some error that will betray a lack of understanding. If you have gone to the trouble of exploring ideas for yourself, then what you write down in the exam room is likely to be a lot more accurate, not to say honest, than any attempt to represent accurately what you have been told in class.
- What you write in the exam will be yours. It will be fresh, engaged, lively and interesting. Imagine the effect it will have on the examiner who has just waded through 20 or so exam scripts that have done nothing more than tediously misrepresent what the candidates have been told by their teacher.

Learning from experience

If you are a student taking GCE Media Studies, you will most likely have taken quite a lot of exams in your school career in order to get to this stage. It is important that you use this experience to help improve your performance in the upcoming exams. So in this section we want you to focus on your previous experience of taking exams and see what you can learn from it.

Think back to the last set of exams that you took. This was probably GCSE. Now ask yourself the following questions.

- Can you remember which exam you performed best in?
- Why was this? (E.g. you liked the subject or the topic you had revised came up)
- How did you prepare for this exam? Did you do anything different from the other exams you sat at that time?
- Were you pleased or disappointed with your result?
- Do you remember the exam you performed worst in?
- Why was this? (E.g. hated the subject or felt really sick on the day)

- How did you prepare for this exam?
- In what way was this exam different from or the same as other exams you sat at that time?
- Were you disappointed with the result or did you expect it?

You may find it useful to share the results of this brief survey with some-one you can talk to, perhaps another student, or a teacher or a relative. What you need to discover is the underlying factors behind your exam perfor-mance. For example, do you perform best in exams where you enjoy the subject? If so, there is a simple logic here, obviously. If, however, you perform best in exams where you don't much like the subject, you need to dig further for possible reasons for this. For example, does the fact that you don't like the subject perversely mean you work harder at it?

You also need to consider what bearing your preparation has on your achievement in the exams you have taken. It is probably worth looking at this over several exams rather than just one, as your performance in one may not be typical. What you should find is that the better your preparation, the better your result. This is, of course, not always the case. Everyone has a story of how they, or their friend, did no work for an exam and ended up with a top grade. These flukes happen, but don't forget that the person telling you this story may not wish you to know just how much they have really prepared for an exam. People like to look cool and unfazed by exams, but often you will find they have been preparing quite hectically in the privacy of their own homes.

The other big question is to consider how you actually approached the exam once you were in the exam room. For example, did you answer all the questions? Did you do the questions in a special order? Were there any other factors that might have helped or hindered your efforts to get a top grade?

Revision

You will know quite some time in advance, usually several months, when you will be taking your exams. This means that you should have ample time to prepare for them. Exam preparation means many different things but perhaps the most important is the need to revise properly. Exam revision is synonymous with late-night poring over textbooks trying to memorise key facts ready for the exam. Media Studies requires you to do little of this, you may be pleased to hear. Although there will be some element of working with textbooks, Media Studies revision should be far more focused on tuning your mind to operate in the right kind of way to perform most effectively in the exams.

Of course, Media Studies revision does share some key strategies with revising for other exams, so it is useful to outline some of these now before looking at the specific revision requirements of AQA Media Studies exams.

The key to effective revision in one word is organisation. If you do not make a serious attempt to get organised, much of your time spent on revision will be completely wasted. Organisation has to start with your class notes. By the time you are reading this, it is likely that a large amount of your note-taking has already been completed. That means that you are likely to have some sorting out to do. If you have not done so already, look at your notes in detail. If your notes are handwritten into a folder, it will probably help to have a large surface area, such as the floor, to use for this purpose. Make sure you will not be disturbed while you are doing this sorting out. Notes are only useful if:

- they make sense
- you can find what you are looking for.

NOTE

Most people use written notes, either in a folder or on a computer. One thing you might like to consider is recording some of your notes on a portable recording device. You can then listen to your notes through headphones when you get a chance and this can be an effective means of helping you remember key information.

Read through all your notes and filter out any that don't make very much sense. Put a note on each page of these notes to remind you what the nature of the problem is – for example, poor handwriting or the fact that you did not understand the topic your notes are intended to cover. Now try to organise the rest into topic areas that you think match in some way the contents of the unit(s) for which you are revising. If you are using an A4 loose-leaf folder, coloured dividers may help you do this. Later in Part 2 where we look at the two exams, we suggest the sorts of headings that you might find useful for organising your notes. Once you have undertaken this basic organisational exercise, it is time to stand back and take stock. One thing that your notes will tell you is what kind of student you are. Here are some suggested adjectives that might be used to describe different approaches to study. Where on the scale for each do you fit?

10		1

Active (see above)	Passive
Organised	Disorganised
Conscientious	Lackadaisical
Thorough	Erratic

With any luck at least some of your responses will place you to the left of the diagram – the virtuous side. If you have put yourself wholly on that side, either you are being dishonest or you need to get a life. What the list should offer you is some sense of your strengths and weaknesses. The very best of students will have weaknesses; the very worst will have some strengths.

This kind of personal audit is called in management-speak a SWOT analysis:

Strengths, Weaknesses, Opportunities and Threats

What a SWOT analysis tries to do is help you identify how you can operate most effectively by playing to your strengths and negating as far as possible your weaknesses. So if you see yourself as an active student with a lively and independent approach to Media Studies but are hopelessly disorganised, then you need to maximise the opportunities presented by the strength you have identified and try to tackle the threat posed by the weakness of being disorganised. This might be simply a matter of teaming up with a fellow student who is organised but generally passive and seeing if you can cooperate with one another to make the best of your skills.

With any luck your notes will be in a condition which is at least serviceable. Unless you are extremely conscientious, there are likely to be gaps. One way to plug these is to enlist the support of other students, perhaps on a swap basis for material that they might need. If all else fails and you think the material you are missing is important to your revision, you will have to get out the necessary textbooks, or visit the appropriate websites and get up to date as best you can. If after doing some chasing in books and talking to other students you still don't understand what may be an important section of your notes, then ask your teacher to help clarify it for you. It may be that you are not the only student in the class who is having difficulty with this topic. This will give the whole class a chance to go over the area again to ensure everyone understands the key details.

NOTE

Time management

This consideration of how important the missing notes are brings to the fore the issue of time management. Ideally the time you spend on any aspect of revision should be proportionate to its significance and value to the exam you are about to take. It would be foolish for example to spend hours or even days chasing information and making notes on some aspect of the course that might not be that important in the exam itself. Equally it would be suicidal not to put effort into some aspect of the course that was absolutely certain to feature as a key element of one or more papers in the exam. The art of time management is to make this kind of judgement so that you optimise your use of the available time.

An essential aspect of time management is the decision you need to take about what to revise. There is clearly an element of judgement about this, not to say that you may also wish to take something of a gamble. The extent to which you choose or need to gamble may well be linked to an equation which puts available time on one side and amount to cover on the other. A lot will depend on how hard you have worked throughout the course.

This is the kind of logical decision that you need to think through in order to make sure that the revision programme that your devise for yourself is as time-efficient as possible. Of course once you have made such a major decision, you need then to put further thought and planning into the more minute detail of your revision.

Once you have got your notes in order and decided precisely what it is you need to revise, the time has come to draw up a plan. Plans of all sorts are an important means of ensuring exam success. A revision plan is designed to help you create a timetable to use to prepare yourself so that you arrive in the exam room ready to put in your best performance. You will no doubt see the parallel with an athlete preparing for an important competition. Just as an athlete does not want 'to peak too soon' or to start their preparation too late, so with an exam revision timetable you need to try to pace your revision to ensure you are at your best on the day of the exam.

So what sort of plan is it you need to draw up? Well, the first decision you need to make is when to start revising. Say you decide that a month before the exam is the right length of time, then you have just over four weeks in which to get yourself prepared. Next you need to decide how much time you can afford to spend revising Media Studies given that you will be revising topics for other subjects at the same time. It may be best to start by thinking of how many hours in each week you think you can afford for your Media Studies revision. Be realistic about this. You may have a part-time job or other demands on your time that will make it difficult to spend the time you would really like to allocate to the subject. It is also best to think in terms of hours for each week because there may be more time at weekends than during a weekday or evening. So you may feel it is easier to have a global amount of time for the week than to try to give a specific amount of time every day.

Once you know how much time you have got, you can proceed to draw up a revision plan. Let us assume that you have decided to revise 30 days before the exam and have allocated an average of one and a half hours a day for your revision. That is a total of 45 hours.

Let us consider how the 45 hours on MEST1 might best be used. As there are two sections to the exam, it makes sense to divide your revision into what is relevant to Sections A and B. As Section A is worth 48 marks and Section B is worth 32 marks, then it would be logical to spend more time revising Section A. It is also the case that the focus of Section A – the key concepts – form the foundation for the cross-media study; therefore a lot of your revision will be relevant to both sections. The following box suggests an approach to organising the time you have for revision.

Section A: Texts, concepts and contexts

20 hours roughly divided between the following concepts:

- Media Forms (media language, genre, narrative)
- Representation
- Audience
- Institution.

Exemplification: Writing practice answers etc. (5 hours): see section on revising Section A for detailed suggestions of exemplification.

Section B: Cross-media study

13 hours to revise cross-media study, including:

- Codes and conventions of a range of products
- Links between the three media platforms
- Key concepts
- Contemporary media debates and issues.

Exemplification: Essay planning and writing (7 hours): see section on revising Section B (p. 74) for detailed suggestions of exemplification.

Remember that your revision plan is just that, a plan, not a legally binding document. Although on one level it is a kind of contract with yourself to do the work you have agreed, it also needs to be flexible enough to be modified if circumstances dictate. For example, you may find that some of the topics you have chosen for revision are more straightforward and hence less time-consuming than you expected. Other areas may demand more of your time. The value of your plan is that it serves as a reminder and a guide that will help you remain on track and, it is hoped, prevent you getting distracted or drifting off at a tangent.

Once you have decided what to revise and allotted the time for revision, you need to consider how you can most effectively get on with the job.

NOTE

Notice how the revision process seems to lend itself to making lists. Making lists is a good way to help get yourself organised and to rationalise what it is you have to do. It is easy to become overwhelmed by what you feel needs to be done. Writing a list is one way to bring some sense of proportion to the task ahead. It also allows you to allocate appropriate amounts of time to each of the items on the list.

One real and unsung benefit of lists is the therapeutic value of crossing off items you have dealt with. When you start making a list, however daunting, just imagine the pleasure you will get when you cross off the last few items. The pleasure can be even greater if you have promised yourself some special treat once the last item has been firmly struck through.

It is important to remember that everyone is different. Consequently there are no hard and fast rules for how best to revise. What matters most is that you find out for yourself a method of revising that is going to be the most effective. You also need to find out a method of revising that makes optimal use of your precious time. Again this means getting organised. It is quite a salutary experience to make an analysis of how you spend your time over a period of a week, broken down in terms of the 168 available hours. A fairly rough breakdown will do. It can be realised in terms of activities such as:

- sleeping
- working (as in paid employment)
- study (in and out of class)
- leisure activities
- travelling.

One thing you will find is that there are periods of time that you simply cannot account for. Try to figure what happens to these and if they may be time you could reclaim to allocate to your revision plan. Another point you need to consider is how you can optimise your use of time – for example, working on the train or bus or using breaks at work or school to do some reading.

Of course this leads to an important issue about finding the most helpful conditions under which to revise. Just as some people have a happy knack of being able to fall asleep anywhere, so some people seem to be able to read, write or research regardless of what is going on around them. Similarly other people need to have everything just right before they can concentrate on any kind of study activity. Most people are somewhere in between, able to tolerate a limited degree of discomfort and distraction. It is worth considering where you might fit on this spectrum, not least in order to help you arrive at some recognition of the most propitious circumstances and environment for revision. For example, you might consider some of the following factors that can influence how effectively you can work:

- Noise. Just how sensitive are you to noise as a source of distraction?
- Hell is other people. How helpful do you find it to be supported by other people? Do you work best on your own or as part of a group of people revising together?
- Attention span. Different people have different attention spans. What is your optimal attention span? Do you start to flag after half an hour and need to do something else for a short while to get your concentration and motivation back? Or can you keep going for a couple of hours especially with the promise of a reward at the end?
- Where is the best place to work to ensure you have access to everything that you need? Remember you may need to use a computer and textbooks as well as your notes.
- Can you get anything useful done in short bursts – for example, on short journeys or during breaks? It is a good idea to make sure you always have something useful to hand such as a textbook when opportunities for short bursts of revision arise.

When you have answered all the above questions, you should be in a position to determine how best to revise. Find the right location where you can work most effectively and as far as possible without distraction or temptation. If this means staying late at school or college or working in the local library, then that is a sacrifice you have to make.

Remember too that the best revision requires you to use the plan you have drawn up in order to plan revision sessions. Regular revision is far more effective for most students than erratic cramming sessions when you seek to cover everything in one marathon period of study. A short burst of focused revision is likely to help you far more, especially if you make sure that this happens at regular intervals – for example, once a day or three times a week. You should certainly think about a diary or a wall planning chart as an aid to planning your revision activities.

Revision tip

It can be easy to think that because you've been sitting for an hour with your notes, past questions and list of areas to revise that you have actually done some revision. Indeed you might have been very productive. However, it is worth asking yourself whether you were really concentrating – how often did you check your phone, or Facebook, or email? Did you have a quick look at a video on YouTube? (Although as this is Media Studies, you could claim that was relevant!)

One strategy for making sure you use your time effectively is to break your revision into periods of 25 minutes, during which time your phone is out of reach, and internet browser and email closed. At the end of 25 minutes (it's best to have a timer for this) you can have a short break of 3 or 4 minutes, and after four sessions take a longer break. A lot of people find this a really helpful technique and it can make you realise how much of your work time you actually spend texting, on social network sites etc.

For more tips on this kind of study see: www.pomodoro technique.com/resources/ pomodoro_cheat_sheet.pdf.

How is GCE (AS) Media Studies different from GCSE?

The AS Media Studies exam is likely to be your first exam since you took your GCSEs. While many of the techniques you used for your Year 11 assessments, such as revision timetables, study skills, essay planning etc., will still be relevant, it is also the case that AS exams represent a step up from GCSE, requiring additional skills and knowledge. This is true for all subjects but we are going to focus specifically on the differences (and similarities) between GCSE and AS Media Studies.

The most striking difference you will find in moving from year 11 to 12 is the level of independence now expected of you. At GCSE the teaching and assessment is tightly focused, often with very clear tasks provided for coursework and controlled assessments. Although this will vary depending on the specification studied, you may have been asked to write a short analysis of a film poster which discussed the target audience. Another task may have focused on the use of narrative within the opening sequence of a TV programme. This approach recognises that at GCSE level you still need – to a greater or lesser extent – quite firm guidance in order to be able to develop your skills in analysis, research and production. At AS it is assumed that these skills – again to a greater or lesser extent! – are in place, which means that you can move on with a greater degree of independence to explore wider contexts.

At GCSE Media Studies the media product (film, TV programme, website, newspaper, etc.) is the primary focus of your research, analysis and production tasks. Although you will also have done some work on industries and audiences, the emphasis is on analysis of the product and your ability to replicate it in production work. At AS the media product is of course still important but there is less emphasis on the analysis of codes and conventions and more interest in what the media product tells you about the role of the media today. This would include thinking about the influence of media industries, the role of public service broadcasting, the effect of new technology on media production and consumption and how the media shapes the way we see and think about ourselves (if you think it does at all).

One of the aims of any A-level course is to help you to develop your research skills, to analyse ideas and to work independently – skills which are invaluable for whatever you decide to do post-A level. At AS these approaches are vital in constructing a successful cross-media study where you will be expected to select your own area to research and to identify the relevant issues and debates.

There are of course also some similarities between GCSE and AS Media Studies which you will find very useful – particularly in the first few weeks of study. You should already be familiar with the key concepts in the subject such as genre, representation, audience and industry as well as some of the specialist terminology associated with Media Studies such as *mise en scène*, codes and conventions, institutions, etc. As an AS student with Media Studies GCSE, you will also probably be familiar with some of the practical production techniques including story boarding and editing; perhaps you have used some of the specialist software programmes such as Adobe Photoshop. All these aspects are valuable in helping you to move on to the next stage of Media Studies.

What if I didn't do GCSE Media Studies?

Many students who take AS Media Studies did not study the subject at GCSE, for a variety of reasons, and you do not need to have taken it to study the subject at AS. In many cases, depending on the type of school or college you're studying at, those without Media Studies GCSE will outnumber those who have it. Your teacher will not assume that all the students will be equally familiar with Media Studies key concepts and terms; instead the first few weeks of the course will form a mini foundation course where these will be introduced (during this time try to ignore the ex-Media Studies GCSE students who seem to know the answer to everything!). Even if you didn't do Media Studies at GCSE it is very likely that you covered relevant material in other courses. For example, in English Language GCSE the study of different types of narrative often includes film examples and newspapers are regularly used to provide examples of different styles of language. Take some time to make a note of any study of the media you did in other subjects – it may reassure you!

> **NOTE**
>
> AS has been described as the level that a student is expected to reach at the end of the first year of an A-level course. It is also intended to reflect a level between GCSE and the standard you should achieve at the end of your GCE course. More recently awarding bodies have begun to talk about 'potential' as a factor in AS performance. What is being measured is the potential of students taking AS level. A question often asked is 'What can we expect of this student when s/he comes to take the A2 examination?'

This has important implications for your approach to the AS exams you are taking. It emphasises even more the importance of trying to showcase your grasp of the Media Studies concepts, theories and ideas you have met in your first year of study. You need to demonstrate your potential by showing how well you have engaged with the subject at this initial level. If you can show sound understanding of the basic ideas that underpin the subject, then you will convince the examiner that in a year's time your understanding will be quite sophisticated. This should have a positive impact on the marks you receive. So a good strategy is to be prepared to be adventurous with your responses. Be prepared to try out ideas and take chances in your answers. This way you will signal to the examiner that you have engaged with and are beginning to show confidence in dealing with Media Studies as a discipline.

In preparing for the AQA Media Studies qualification, you will encounter one external exam, split into two sections each different in approach. Section A requires you to write about an unseen media product, while Section B requires you to write an essay response. Despite the different approaches required by these sections, they do have quite a lot in common and to some extent require a similar approach on your part. Both are 'enabling' exams, in keeping with an established tradition in terms of Media Studies assessment.

What we mean by 'enabling' is that they are designed to allow the candidate to show off what they have learned rather than seeking to expose weaknesses in candidates' understanding and skills. A particularly useful way to consider the two Media Studies AS exams is to look at them in this way:

- Your Media Studies course should have given you a set of skills. Your job in the exams is to show what you have learned.
- In the course of your study, you have engaged with a range of media products across different media forms. Your job in the exam is to demonstrate that you have learned to apply what you have learned to these products and others like them.

As you should have realised, the emphasis at AS level is on analysis. You need to feel confident about applying your analytical skills both to the unseen product you will encounter in Section A and to products you have already explored ready for the exam. This focus on the analysis has an important bearing on how you prepare for and approach the AS exams.

A very real issue for the student of Media Studies is that the paper that you sit at AS level could be attempted by someone who had never been to a Media Studies class. The media are an important element of the culture of this country and in consequence they impact on the lives of us all. In consequence everyone is likely to have some view on the many issues raised by the media we are all exposed to. It is hard to travel on public transport or sit in a café without someone expressing their views on the latest reality TV show. Indeed the questions set in Section B might well serve as the opening gambit in a pub conversation.

That does of course raise the question: why bother doing a Media Studies course if anyone can attempt the questions? The answer of course is quite a simple one. A media course will give you a conceptual understanding and analytical skills that an uninformed person off the street could not hope to have. It should also be a signal for you to realise that in order to do well in AS Media Studies exams you need to demonstrate to the examiner that you do have conceptual understanding and analytical skills and above all that you know how to apply these. The key to success is to know how best to do this.

If you eavesdrop on people's conversations on public transport for example, you will find that the media offer many opportunities for discussion. References to media issues, last night's television, the latest tabloid revelations about a celebrity scandal or the battle for the number one single slot at Christmas are an important lubricant in our social interaction. Most members of the public could offer you an interpretation of an unseen product, a magazine cover or advertisement or a film sequence for example, simply by explaining what it means to them. So how might a Media Studies examiner discriminate between such lay opinions and the responses of a student who has followed a Media Studies course? The answer to this question provides an important key to success for the student taking Media Studies exams. What examiners are most eager to find in your response is clear evidence that a candidate has engaged fully and effectively in a study of the media. This evidence can be demonstrated in a variety of ways, but two particular aspects of a response would be especially compelling:

- *Conceptual understanding*. Media Studies, as you should be aware, has an important conceptual framework. This means that there is a set of concepts in the form of ideas and theories that inform our understanding of media products, issues and debates. These ideas are academic concepts that place a study of the media within a framework that enables an exploration of media ideas to take place with some degree of consensus between the participants in this exploration. This approach assumes, for example, that when we comment on a media issue we have some awareness of academic writing and research previously undertaken into this issue. This means that a student of media is likely to speak with significantly more authority than a lay person for the simple reason that they will have this awareness of previous study that has taken place into the topic.
- *Discourse*. Media Studies as an academic discipline has its own discourse. Discourse is itself an academic term derived from linguistics. It describes the language which a discipline uses to discuss its subject matter. So the discourse of Media Studies requires you to utilise appropriately specific technical terms when you explore issues and debates within the discipline. For example, if you are travelling home on the bus, you might hear someone say, 'These reality TV shows are really mind-numbing.' If their travelling companion replies, 'Yes, it is also a genre which raises a number of ideological issues', you might conclude that while the first speaker is a clued-in lay person, the second has followed some sort of Media Studies programme. The first speaker is expressing an informed viewpoint using everyday language, while the second is using a technical vocabulary expressed within the discourse of Media Studies. You may also note that the view of the second speaker seems to carry rather more weight because it is expressed in a discourse that suggests they have some knowledge and authority within the discipline.

AS Media Studies: a brief overview

AS unit outline

The AS Media Studies course is designed to guide you in investigating the media in order to understand and evaluate how meanings and responses are created by a range of media products. These products are studied in the context of the contemporary media landscape and a range of issues and debates. Students on the AS Media Studies course should be independent in research and production skills as well as in developing their own views and reputations.

Both units are structured around key media concepts and media platforms:

- The media concepts

    - Media forms (media language, narrative and genre)
    - Media representations
    - Media institutions
    - Media audiences

- The media platforms

    - Broadcasting
    - Digital/Web-based media
    - Print

UNIT 1 – MEST1: INVESTIGATING MEDIA

The focus of MEST1: Investigating Media is the analysis of media products within the wider contexts of audience, institution and representation in order to examine how meaning and response are created. This unit requires skills of analysis as well as an understanding of wider issues and debates.

MEST1 assessment
MEST1 is 50% of AS, 25% of A level
Two hour written examination: 80 marks

The exam is in two parts:

- Section A (48 marks) – unseen product (moving image, print, digital technology) with four compulsory short answer questions on media forms, audiences, representation and institution.
- Section B (32 marks) – one essay from a choice of two, based on your cross-media study.

UNIT 2 – MEST2: CREATING MEDIA

Creating Media is the practical, coursework unit in which you will produce two linked pieces of production work from two of the three media platforms studied in MEST 1. In addition you will also produce a 1,500 word evaluation which outlines your aims and research. The production pieces are produced in response to a brief provided by the exam board.

MEST2 assessment

MEST2 is 50% of AS, 25% of A level

Practical unit, internally assessed by your teacher and externally moderated by the exam board: 80 marks

Two linked production pieces (60 marks) plus 1,500-word evaluation (20 marks).

How assessment is weighted

Media studies – like every other subject – is structured around a list of aims. These are the things which the awarding body thinks you should be able to do as an AS and then an A2 student. They are called Assessment Objectives (AOs). The four in Media Studies are:

- AO1 Demonstrate knowledge and understanding of media concepts, contexts and critical debates.
- AO2 Apply knowledge and understanding when analysing media products and processes and evaluating practical work, to show how meanings and responses are created.
- AO3 Demonstrate the ability to plan and construct media products using appropriate technical and creative skills.
- AO4 Demonstrate the ability to undertake, apply and present appropriate research.

Take a moment to study these AOs and think about how they link to your AS studies.

- Which AOs apply to MEST1?
- Which AOs refer to MEST2?
- What overlap is there between the two units in terms of the types of skills – analysis, evaluation, planning, technical etc. – being assessed?

Understanding how the exam board weights the AOs in relation to the units can help you to focus on the specific skills you need to demonstrate. Looking at the table below it is clear that in the MEST1 exam it is the ability to demonstrate knowledge of specific media products and the wider media contexts in which they exist which is important.

Table 1 *Exam board weighting for AOs*

Assessment Objectives	MEST1 weighting (%)	MEST2 weighting (%)
AO1	30	0
AO2	20	10
AO3	0	30
AO4	0	10

A02, which accounts for 20% of the examined unit MEST1, is also assessed in your coursework unit, MEST2. This suggests that there may be aspects of your coursework which will help you in preparing for the exam.

What have I learned in MEST2 that I can use in MEST1?

Thinking about any overlap between the two units is a different way to approach your revision for the exam which (particularly if you feel that you are better at the technical and creative aspects of the course than the more theoretical ones) you may find more accessible in the initial stages of exam preparation.

Use the following bullet points as prompts and relate each to your own examples from your coursework.

Revision tip

Before starting to look back over MEST2, make sure you have any notes and planning you did, perhaps in the form of a log or diary, as well as a copy of your written evaluation, if you have completed it.

- How are production skills and the theoretical approaches needed for the exam linked?
- Think about the relevant research and planning you had to do before constructing your products:

  - Analysis of existing products (films, adverts, posters, games, newspapers, etc.) in terms of their codes and conventions (media language, genre and narrative) in order to replicate these in your own product.
  - Carrying out audience research into a range of existing products to understand how they use particular modes of address.

- Thinking about how to address a specific audience with your product should help you gain a deeper understanding about how existing media speak to particular audiences.

- Closely linked to mode of address is the issue of representation. In addition to analysing different types of representation, the process of selection and construction of representation in your own work will develop your knowledge of how representations function in the media.
- Working to a brief which is based on industry practice develops your understanding of the context in which the product will be distributed and consumed, information which can be used in discussing the role of institutions.
- Producing work across two platforms means that you should have a good understanding of the way in which products are produced and distributed across platforms and the reasons for this.
- The written evaluation of your products has many similarities to both sections of MEST1 in that you are analysing the products in the context of the key concepts.

> **NOTE**
>
> Remember – you cannot use your own media products as examples for your cross-media study: the products there have to be examples of professional practice produced by media institutions.

Help!

So you have completely screwed things up. You are going into an exam tomorrow with only minimal preparation. The best you feel you can do is to write your name on the paper and leave as soon as the invigilator will let you go. Well, you don't have too much going for you. There is, however, a chance you can salvage something from this disaster. First, spend a little time figuring how this situation came about. How much of it is your fault? How much is due to circumstances over which you feel you have little or no control? OK, so there is little you can do about it now, but at least you can make sure you are forearmed and better prepared next time.

The next thing is to make a fast audit of what you do know. Make a list of the key concepts (see p. 57) and try to write a brief summary next to each or some of the key bits of information you need to be able use in the exam. You should know by now, or at least your teacher should, whether it is a moving image or print product that you are going to be confronted with. So if it is a moving image, you might like to write down:

'Media Language: type of shot, type of edit, narrative, genre, etc.'

Do the same for all the other key concepts, most especially the four important ones.

If you have time, have a quick practice run on something such as a film trailer or a television advertisement which you have recorded and just try to get down some notes under the key concepts.

Finally learn some terminology. You should know terms for the way in which you will want to describe shots and edits in the sequence.

If all else fails, remember that unless you are a serial screwer-up of exams, there should be another chance in a year's time and perhaps you will have sorted yourself out and feel better prepared next time.

Section B of MEST1 is going to pose you a rather bigger problem unfortunately. Winging it on the day is going to be a lot more difficult than it is with Section A. The reason for this is that you need to have something prepared in your head to take into the exam. Specifically you need some kind of case study with good examples that you can use to exemplify some of the conceptual issues that the exam may focus on. The one thing that you have going for you, however, is potentially a really big advantage. The Section B part of the exam demands an engagement for the most part with contemporary media output. If you sort this out the night before the exam, that is about as contemporary as you can get. So this is how you might go about trying to salvage something from Section B.

First, check out what you know. Presumably you have been to some classes and have some notes and perhaps have read some bits of textbooks. Try to make some headings around what you know. For example, you might use the key concepts yet again as headings for this. The other key issue is what topic you are going to write about. Once you have your topics sorted out, you need to find examples to use to support your answers in the exam. (See the section on revising Section B (p. 74) for advice on which topics work well for rapid revision.)

A couple of hours of study on each with close application of the key concepts and you should be able to pop into the exam tomorrow and get a decent grade! Well, probably not, but if the wind is in the right direction and your good luck charms all work, you might just pass.

Of course, you will have realised by this point that it would have been better to have prepared properly and not put yourself under all this pressure. So it goes.

Making examiners happy

All examiners are expected to read each of your answers carefully in order to award marks. You can make it easier for the examiner by paying careful attention to how your script looks when the examiner gets to see it. You will help your own cause a good deal if you make sure of the following:

- Write clearly and as legibly as possible. Having a good pen with black ink is essential. If your handwriting is truly awful, consider printing.
- Read the instructions on the front of the exam paper carefully. Make it absolutely clear which question you are answering. It is a good idea to start each new question on a new page of your exam booklet.
- Clearly indicate the question by writing the number of the question – for example, 3a – in the margin or writing out the question in full.
- Paragraph your work properly. This helps break up your answer into logical sections. A whole page of handwriting with no breaks is a daunting prospect for even the most seasoned of examiners.
- Avoid using correcting fluid (not allowed by awarding bodies because it sticks pages together) and pens other than black.
- Use helpful signposts for the examiner – for example, put quotes on a separate line.

MEST1 INVESTIGATING MEDIA SECTION A: ANALYSIS OF AN 'UNSEEN' MEDIA PRODUCT

Assessment at a glance: Section A

- Section A is based on your response to an unseen product which you will see as part of the exam.
- It assesses ability in demonstrating knowledge and understanding of media concepts, contexts and critical debates.
- Answer all four questions.
- Section A is worth 48 marks.
- You should spend approximately 1 hour and 15 minutes on planning and writing your responses to the questions in Section A. This includes 15 minutes of viewing or reading time for the product.
- The answer booklet gives you pages for notes and two sides to answer each of the four questions.
- Section A assesses AO2, which is the ability to apply knowledge and understanding when analysing media products and processes to show how meanings and responses are created.
- The questions are designed to:

  - assess candidates' ability to apply their knowledge and understanding of the products and processes of the unseen product
  - explore how meanings and responses are created.

- As indicated within each level, Quality of Written Communication is taken into account.

What's the point of analysing an unseen media product?

Media output is generally intended for mass consumption. It exists to be consumed. Most of the time it will be consumed quickly and without very much thought. In consequence, unless it is in some way special, it doesn't get considered very much at all, let alone written about, except perhaps when selected for review in other areas of the media or for the purposes of academic study. The idea behind analysis, which is what this section is about, is to get you to take a considered and close look at a specific media product or part of one. In doing so you are invited to bring to that product your expertise in applying the conceptual framework you have developed in studying the media.

Activity

Some media products are more open to scrutiny than others. For example, films are reviewed in specialist print and online magazines, on fan sites, on television and radio and in the press. What do you think is the function of these reviews? Do they influence you? Do they enhance your enjoyment of media consumption? Have you ever come across the analysis of a media product in a textbook or on a website that you feel has enriched your experience of consuming the media?

So, analysing media products is a basic skill you need to master in your study of the media. It encourages detailed consideration of media products. The ability to consider in depth and respond to a product by applying these analytical skills is a cornerstone of successful study of the media at this level.

NOTE

The reason that the product is unseen is also important. On a simple level, making it unseen creates some kind of level playing field for everyone taking the exam. All candidates will start from the same position, unlike a situation where you may have been given time before the exam to prepare a response with the help of an array of friends, family and even teachers. On a more complex level, a good candidate should be able to think on their feet. If you have really taken in and understood the concepts that underpin your AS course, you should have grown proficient at analysing a whole range of different types and forms of media products. So being confronted by one unseen in an exam should be pretty straightforward.

NOTE

As you know, in the AQA specification these skills of analysis are tested particularly in Section A of the exam where students have to analyse a previously unseen product in exam conditions. However, the skills employed here are also applied in using detailed examples (Section B) and in the supporting written elements of MEST2 (the practical production), where you are required to analyse and evaluate a product you have created. At A2 level these skills remain crucially important. Therefore, it is clear that your ability to analyse it effectively and in detail impacts significantly upon your success within the qualification as a whole.

Analytical skills

Section A comes at the beginning of the MEST1 paper. When you take the exam, it makes a lot of sense for many reasons to do that section first.

Reasons for doing Section A first:

- Your answers to this section rely on your response to an unseen product. If it is a moving image product, then you will want to write your answers to the questions while the product is still fresh in your mind.
- Section A is worth more marks than Section B, so it makes sense to ensure that you give it an appropriate amount of time and focus.
- Section A is more complex than Section B as there will be a greater need to organise your response under the headings of four separate questions.

So what is involved in Section A? Well, it is worth 48 of the 80 marks available on the paper. These marks are awarded through four questions each worth 12 marks. The questions are based on your analysis of a product that you will probably see for the first time in the exam. This may take the form of:

- A print product which will be included as part of the exam paper issued to you. This is usually produced in the form of an insert or additional sheet folded into your paper. It is likely to be a close reproduction of an original print product such as an advertisement, film poster or an extract from a newspaper or magazine.
- A moving image product in the form of a DVD which will be played to you three times in order to give you the opportunity to study it thoroughly before writing your answer. The movie image product may take a variety of forms, such as a television advertisement, a film or television programme trailer or the opening sequence of a programme.
- An e-media product which may take the form of a print-out of a website for example, or perhaps a DVD presentation of a YouTube video.
- The possibility of another media format such as a radio extract, although to date only examples from the first three categories have been set.

What to expect if the Section A product takes the form of a DVD

The DVD with the moving image product will be played to you at the start of the exam. It will probably be shown on a television with a large enough screen to ensure everyone can see and hear it clearly. The DVD comes in a standard version and one with subtitles, for the use of hard-of-hearing candidates. The invigilator will start the DVD and then pause it to make sure everyone can see and hear OK. If you can't do one or the other, speak up so the problem can be sorted.

The invigilator then re-starts the DVD and runs it through without pausing again to the end. This takes about 15 minutes.

A voice-over will tell you precisely what is happening but it is important to take note of the following:

- The product will be shown to you three times with pauses of around 3 to 5 minutes in between showings.
- A tone will sound to warn you when each showing of the product is about to begin.
- It is best not to make notes on the first showing but rather to watch it to get an overview of what it is and how you respond to it.
- Be ready to make notes on the second and third viewing. Detailed information about what sort of notes to make is given on p. 42.

Revision tip

There is an outside chance you may have come across the product before, either because your teacher has used it in class, not knowing of course that it will be set for the exam, or simply as part of your general media consumption. Obviously, if you have seen it before that is hugely reassuring but do bear in mind that when you view it in the exam, your focus needs to be on the specific questions you are being asked. Don't confuse this with a more general response you might have had when you saw it previously. As you will discover many times in this book, question focus is extremely important.

Revision tip

Question focus is an important concept in taking exams. It means basically answering the question you have been asked. This may sound simple but examiners find an awful lot of students when they attempt a question provide an answer which they have either pre-prepared or one that they find easier than the question set. Good candidates focus on the question and use what they have learned to provide a specific answer to the specific question.

Once you have viewed the product and made your notes, you must then attempt the four questions which have been asked about the product. These questions are each under the heading of the four key concepts that are being tested in this paper:

1   Media Forms
2   Media Representations
3   Media Institutions
4   Media Audiences

These headings appear with a question on each but the order in which they are presented may vary from year to year. A detailed discussion of these concepts can be found on p. 57.

The four questions in Section A are known to examiners as short answer questions. This differentiates them from the longer essay-style question you will tackle in Section B. They are short in order to focus you and test you on specific concepts and detail related to the product you are asked to analyse.

You are advised on the front of the exam paper to spend 1 hour and 15 minutes on this section of the paper. This includes 15 minutes of viewing or reading time, so you are looking at around 15 minutes to write an answer to each of the four questions. Spending an equal amount of time on each is quite important as you will see on p. 44.

Revision tip

As you know, you will be required to answer the questions in a specially designed answer booklet that has the questions printed in it. This means that there is a specific amount of space for you to attempt each of the Section A questions. This is two sides of A4 with about 25 lines on each. Obviously some handwriting is larger than others, but as a rough guide there should be enough space here for you to fully answer each question. If you do need more space, then you can use the space indicated in your answer booklet. However, in general, if you need more than the space provided it is likely that you are writing too much on a specific question and you might be better moving on to the next one rather than writing on additional sheets.

What is Section A all about/what are examiners looking for?

On the front of the MEST1 question paper, which few candidates ever bother to read, is a useful insight into what is being tested by the paper and by implication what examiners are looking for in your answers. In the section headed 'Information', you will see the following bullet points:

You will be expected to show that you know and understand:

meaning
How a media product is interpreted by an audience.

responses
How audiences react to a media product often on an emotional level – e.g. 'I loved that film; it made me cry.'

- Media concepts, contexts and critical debates
- How meanings and responses are created within media products and processes.

Activity

Write down a paragraph for each of the above explaining what you think it tells you about how to tackle Section A.

So what does it mean? Check your ideas with the ones that follow. Note that you need both to 'know and understand'. So in your answers you must demonstrate not only your awareness of these ideas but also show you understand them. The evidence of your understanding them is through showing you are able to apply them to the analysis of the unseen product you are confronted with.

Let's look at each of the expectations in turn.

media contexts
Refers to the ways in which media products are created and consumed.

Media concepts, contexts and critical debates. Concepts clearly refers here to the key concepts that you are being asked to apply in your response to the unseen product. Conveniently, the questions set are under the headings of these concepts: Media Forms, Media Representations, Media Institutions and

Media Audiences. As you will see later, an important aspect of demonstrating your understanding of these concepts is your ability to separate them from one another.

Contexts are important in exploring any media output. Two contexts are particularly important: production and consumption. Production contexts relate closely to the concept of institutions as they are concerned with where media products come from and how they are created. Consumption contexts are at the other end of process. These concern the concept of how Media Audiences are related to the way in which media products are consumed and how audiences use media products.

Critical debates are a bit more complex and in some ways have more application to Section B. However, in the context of Section A they relate to those contentious issues that surround the production and consumption of the media. The critical debates are likely to vary according to the products set. For example, an extract from a reality television programme might raise critical debates about voyeurism in the media. The front page of a newspaper might raise issues about press ethics or the survival of print media in an age of digital technology. Obviously your awareness of critical debates will be enhanced by your engagement with media issues which you should have come across as part of your studies.

media debates
Issues in the media about which people disagree.

How meanings and responses are created within media products and processes. This second bullet point obviously has a direct application to Section A. The focus of this section is analysis, specifically the type of analysis which enables us to understand how a media product is created in order to elicit from the audience a response which in turn enables them to interpret the product and understand its meaning. As you will see later, it is your ability to show that you understand the process by which a media product conveys its meaning to the audience that is likely to get you a good mark in this section. It is, however, important that you accept that different audiences are likely to interpret products in different ways and that whilst your own response and interpretation of a product is important, they are more than likely not the only way of seeing it.

Activity

Imagine AQA have set the opening sequence of a crime drama set in an inner-city police station in the UK as the product for analysis. The exam is being sat by a group of police recruits and a group of criminals. How do you think the two groups might interpret the sequence differently?

How Section A is organised

Section A of the MEST1 paper has been organised to be as user-friendly as possible. You will find the background information about the product and the four questions you are asked all together often on one side of the question paper. The format for responding to the questions is in the form of an answer booklet with each of the questions printed again at the top of a section. Usually a couple of sides are reserved for your response. As we said earlier, these two sides should be just about sufficient for a person with average handwriting to get down a response in the time allocated. If you do need to go on to an additional sheet, make sure that:

- you are not repeating yourself
- you are not using time that should be given to another question.

Note that the front of the question paper advises you that you need to use 'good' English and organise relevant information clearly. Obviously this applies to the longer essay questions in Section B but you should also bear in mind that it is relevant to this section as well. What you need to do now is to transform your notes into a well-organised and well-written response to each of the questions. You can tackle the issue of organisation directly from your notes. If you have numbered your ideas for each section as suggested above, this should give you the ideal organisational structure for a response to each section. So your format should be along the lines of:

exemplification
The process of illustrating or proving your point by providing a relevant example.

- point 1
- exemplification from product
- point 2
- further exemplification product.

Repeat the process for the number of points you want to make.

> **NOTE**
>
> How many points should I make for each question? Well, usefully the mark scheme differentiates between candidates who achieve the top level (10 to 12 marks) by their referring to a wide range of points relevant to the question being asked. At the lower end of the mark scheme, examiners are just looking for 'some' of these points. While this does not give you a numerical answer, it should indicate that more points made is better than fewer. If you think of trying to get down about four appropriate and well-made points, each supported by detailed evidence, you should be heading in the right direction. Fewer than four points are probably not enough; too many more are going to dilute what you have to say a bit too much.

Getting started with Section A

In this section we look at how best to approach Section A once you are in the exam room.

You should know something of what to expect before you actually go into the exam room as your school or college will have had prior warning if the exam will require the use of DVD playback facilities. Your teacher will be able to pass this information on to you prior to the exam. Obviously if a DVD is required, you can expect some form of audio-visual product such as a moving image sequence. Otherwise you are likely to be dealing with print-based media. In either case you will still have 15 minutes of viewing/reading time before you start writing your responses to the questions. Learning to use this time effectively is one of the keys to success in this part of the exam. So how do you do this?

The approach to moving image products is likely to be different from the way you would approach a print product. Let's have a look at the moving image product first.

It is probably worth checking through quickly the section on p. 36 which deals with the mechanics of showing a moving image product in the exam so you fully understand what is involved. It will also help you decide on what strategy is going to be best for you if you are going to get the most out of the three separate viewings of the product. Different students may find they each benefit from a slightly different approach. A lot depends on how quickly you take things in and how good you are at recalling detail that you have seen when the product is shown.

Tackling a moving image product in the exam

As you are aware, the moving image will be shown to you three times with a time gap in between each showing. If you are going to do well in this section of the paper, you need to know how best to use the time spent on the three screenings. Obviously every student is different, so there is no one-size-fits-all approach to how to do this. If you have developed a system that works well for you, then don't change it. However, there are some fundamental aspects of tackling moving image that will work for most students. Consider these and be prepared to modify them according to your own needs and approach.

The first thing to do before you are shown the product is to take the opportunity to look at the questions in Section A. Be sure to read the questions carefully and think about the focus of each one. For example, the question on Media Forms might ask you to consider narrative or *mise en scène*. If this is the case, bear this in mind when you have your first viewing of the product. Then, if you have time, read through the information given to you about the product. Reading through the questions is most important at this stage so be sure to do that. During the first viewing of the product, try to take in as much as you can. Sometimes it will feel as though there is almost too much to absorb. Don't worry at this stage, just try to get as detailed an impression as you can and do so with the focus of the four questions you have read in mind.

Activity

Get yourself used to viewing short sequences of moving images lasting a couple of minutes or so. When you have finished viewing them, try to recall them as they relate to the four key concept headings that form the exam questions. If you are able to, try jotting down your thoughts under each heading, or use the voice recorder on your phone to make a note of them. This is a great way of making you think automatically in terms of the key concepts.

NOTE

www.youtube.com

www.bbc.co.uk/learningz
one/clips

http://uk.filmtrailer.com

www.tellyads.com

The Web provides plenty of opportunities for you to find short examples of moving image products that you can use to hone your analysis skills in preparation for moving image in the exam. One obvious example is YouTube. You do need to be careful, however, that you select primarily broadcast clips to consider, rather than home-produced materials. A really useful site is the BBC Learning Zone Broadband. This site has lots of clips from BBC programmes, many of them about the right length for MEST1 analysis. There are lots of media-specific clips to be found by navigating to Secondary then Media Studies. Film trailer sites are another useful source of short clips for you to play with. Similarly sites featuring television advertisements can be a rich source of appropriate clips.

Immediately the first showing has finished, get yourself into note-taking mode. There are blank sheets especially provided for you to work on your notes inside the MEST1 answer booklet. One good way to approach the note-taking is to divide these pages into four using an abbreviated heading for each of the concepts: MF, Rep, Inst and Aud. It will also help you keep focused if you choose a keyword from each of the questions and write this beneath the headings, For example, under the heading for Audience you might add the word 'appeal' if the question relates to how the product is designed to please or attract an audience. There's an example of how to do this on p. 47.

Having had your first viewing of the product and having created a grid for your notes, make an initial stab at organising your initial responses to the product under the appropriate headings.

Exam tip

Remember your notes will not be marked, so don't worry about making mistakes at this stage. Just use the space to get down your ideas as clearly as possible or at least sufficiently clearly for you to understand them later.

OK, time for the second viewing. During this viewing, see if you can write and view at the same time – a difficult skill, but not impossible. This second viewing is your main chance to home in on and develop your ideas by getting down notes which are detailed and accurate. One quality examiners are looking for in your response is your ability to support your ideas with evidence from the product. This second viewing should provide the opportunity to note down any particular aspects of the product you want to use as supporting evidence in your answers. This means looking for good examples to support the ideas you want to express.

Exam tip

While producing evidence from the product to support your response is important, it is also essential that you don't go off at a tangent describing the product in detail. Try to make notes that will remind you of brief examples rather than whole sequences you might be tempted to describe.

So now you have another time gap to refine and develop your notes. How best to use this is an important decision. Our suggestions would be:

•   Spend a bit of time ensuring that what you have written makes sense and will be usable when you come to write up your responses.
•   Check that you have fairly even coverage across the four key concepts. If one section looks at all short, spend a bit of time to decide what is lacking.

- Make sure your notes link as closely as possible to the question you are being asked in each section. Good notes will focus closely on the keyword you have used under each concept heading.
- Ensure you have a note of the examples you want to use.
- Within each section start to prioritise and order the points in each section. You can do this by numbering each of the points you want to make in the order you think is best.

Time for the third viewing. This viewing should be your opportunity to finesse your notes and get ready to write your response. If there are any deficiencies evident from the bullet point list for the second viewing, make it a priority to address them now. For example, if you have uneven coverage of the concepts, get focused on viewing the product with an eye to addressing this by paying special attention to that particular concept in relation to the product. Similarly if a point you want to make lacks a good example, try to find one during this third viewing.

Exam tip

The key to success in this section is even coverage of the key concepts. Don't make brilliant and exhaustive notes on a couple of the concepts at the expense of the other two. Four responses that each give you eight marks (32 marks) is better than two that each give ten and two that each give you three (26 marks). There is the potential for this to represent a whole grade difference in the result you achieve for this unit.

Tackling a print product in the exam

Suppose you get a print product in the paper you sit. Your approach to responding to a print product is bound to be different from the demands of looking at and responding to an on-screen product. The main difference of course is that you will have the print product available to you throughout the exam. Clearly this is in some ways an advantage over just being able to see it for three short screenings but you also need to be aware that there are disadvantages too. Chief of these is that you may be tempted to spend too much time focused on the product and not enough time getting on with the job of answering the questions.

In order to get the balance right, it is probably best to adopt a similar strategy to the one outlined above for the moving image product. So as soon as you open the exam paper, do the following:

1   Look at the questions that have been set and divide your page for making notes into the key concept sections with a keyword from each section.
2   Read the information provided on the exam paper about the product.
3   Explore the product itself in the same way that you might for any print product you have just picked up and read to give yourself a general sense of what it is about and what your first impressions of it are.

The above equates to the first viewing you might have made of a DVD.

Exam tip

When looking at a print product it is important that you keep your eye on the clock. As you will have seen, the moving image analysis provides a framework for exploring the product and the questions by breaking the time into segments and warning you when each is completed. For print you need to do this for yourself.

Try to get down some initial notes under the appropriate concept headings from your first scrutiny of the product. These first impressions can be especially valuable.

Now recheck the questions so you are fully aware of what the focus is and what you should be looking for. After this make a detailed scrutiny of the product. It is probably best to do this concept by concept. You should aim to complete each of the sections in your notes one at a time. Don't forget to look for:

- the point you want to make
- the evidence in the product to support it.

If you do this for each of the concepts in turn, you should end up with a fairly detailed set of notes. The next job is to check that all the points you make are in the appropriate place. You need to check this carefully as you are not going to get any reward if, for example, you make a really good point about Audience but have placed it under the heading of Representation.

When you have completed this check, try numbering the points in each section in order to prioritise them. You can do this by allocating each point a number to indicate the order in which you think they are best placed in the answer itself.

> ## Exam tip
>
> How best to prioritise. You might be wondering what the best way is of
> prioritising the points you want to make. There is not necessarily a right answer
> to this one. Obviously what you consider to be a major point needs to take
> precedence over a minor point, but in general it is probably best to elect for the
> order you feel most confident about. So start with the point which in your view
> you can write about with the greatest skill and confidence.

Now is the time to keep your eye on the clock. Have you used the whole
15 minutes of reading time you are given for this exploration of the print
product? If you have worked efficiently, there is a good chance you will have
a minute or two left. One option is simply to start work on the answers. A
better option is to have a final look at the product, the questions and the
information about the products on the question paper. Check that:

- you have not missed any vital points
- you have evidence in the form of examples to support the points you do
  make
- you are not repeating material that you have read in the information on
  the paper
- you have even coverage of the key concepts

If all of these things are in place, you are ready to starting writing up your
responses.

A look at the Section A questions in January 2011 MEST1

The product used on this occasion was a moving image product in the form
of a video available on YouTube which was a viral advertisement for the
Mini Clubman car. You can find the product itself by linking to this URL:
www.youtube.com/watch?v=s9UlaKOIdZg. Once you have established the
link, you can try watching it 'under exam conditions' by running it through
three times in 15 minutes as though you were in the exam itself.

The paper provided the following information about the product:

You are about to see the viral video *Have you seen that?* developed by
the German advertising agency 19:13 to launch the new Mini Clubman
car. The advert was released on the internet via YouTube on 25 March

2009. In its first year it had over 180,000 hits as well as being spread further across the internet.

Viral marketing describes any strategy that encourages individuals to pass on a marketing message to others, creating the potential for rapid growth in the message's exposure and influence. A viral video is a video clip that gains widespread popularity through the process of internet sharing, typically through e-mail or instant messaging, blogs and other media sharing websites.

The advertising agency 19:13 was given the demanding brief of creating an exciting video which would go viral and also help to rebrand the Mini Clubman car. The Head of Global Marketing at Mini claimed that 'The viral video demonstrates in an entertaining way what the new Mini Clubman is capable of, and how much pleasure it is driving it. 19:13 implemented that in a literally breathtaking way.'

The questions were as follows:

1   Media Forms: How is the video constructed to engage the audience? (12 marks)
2   Media Institutions: How is the brand image of the Mini Clubman pro- moted in the video? (12 marks)
3   Media Representations: How is the video represented as being real? (12 marks)
4   Media Audiences: What features of the video encourage the audience to pass on the marketing message to others? (12 marks)

So you remember that the first thing you need to do is divide sheets of plain A4 paper into each of the key concept headings. It is probably best to use two sheets, if available, as this will give you around half a side for notes on each of the concepts. Remember you also need to tease out words from each of the questions to help you focus your notes under each of the headings.

Activity

Before you read on, write down the keywords from each question that you would choose to help you focus your notes.

Question 1 (Media Forms) is about how the video is constructed, which potentially allows you to write quite broadly about the production techniques being used in making the video. What focuses and narrows the question is that it is about how the video has been constructed to engage the audience. So the words 'engage audience' would be a useful reminder under the headings of Media Forms.

Question 2 (Media Institutions) asks about the brand image of the Clubman car and how it is promoted in the video. This is very much in marketing and promotion territory rather than more traditional ideas of media institutions and producers. The words 'brand' and 'promoted' would be helpful in focusing your response here.

Question 3 (Media Representations) asks you to consider how the video is represented as being 'real'. The word 'real' would probably suffice to help you with your notes under this concept.

Question 4 (Media Audiences) is an interesting question that invites you to look at the ways in which audiences are active in using media products by passing them on to other people. The words 'pass on' and 'message' should serve as a useful reminder of what this question is asking.

What useful information do you get from the background information to the product provided on the question paper?

Activity

Read the information through and try to pick out the keywords or produce a brief summary of what you think are the important bits of information. Also think about how each piece of information might relate to each of the questions.

The key bits of information you select may be as follows:

- It was created by an advertising agency to promote a new car (Q2).
- It was very popular on YouTube (Q4).
- Viral marketing is about sharing via the Web (Q2 and Q4).
- The agency designed the video to go viral (Q1, Q2 and Q4).
- The video is designed to be entertaining (Q1 and Q4).

NOTE

Reminder: the background information is designed to help you understand the context in which the product has been produced and is likely to be consumed. Avoid simply repeating this information in your answers. You obviously won't get any marks for doing so. Do, however, read it carefully so that you understand this important background detail and see how it might help you respond to the questions.

So what kind of notes would you hope to get down based on your viewings? Remember you are also looking for examples from the product to support each of your ideas, so try to make a note of them as well. Let's have a look question by question:

Question 1: Media Forms – engage audience

The first point that may strike you is the positioning of the audience in this clip. The point-of-view shot is a powerful technique to engage audiences by putting them right alongside the action. In this case we are placed inside the car alongside the driver and passenger. We see what they see; the camera shot takes us to the heart of the action. To support your point you might give the example of the voyeuristic way in which the audience is invited to witness and marvel the death-defying antics of the Mini drivers that we are following. They have in fact a ringside seat.

The second point might be to consider the authenticity of the video. Real or fake is obviously a key enigma confronting us, the audience. Certainly there is evidence that it looks real, such as the interior of the car and the realistic images of the motorway. The blokes in the car sound like ordinary blokes reacting to an extraordinary event. The scene does, however, also have the sense of being part of a video game where we, the players, are offered the point of view of the screen as we take part in it.

Humour is also used as a tool to engage the audience. We eavesdrop on the dialogue of the two men in the car. (What is the in-joke about Rimini?) We are invited to laugh at their attempts to rationalise what is going on until they finally conclude they have been had: it's a fake.

Activity

Choose a couple of examples of humour in the dialogue that you think might exemplify the way it is used to engage the audience.

Finally there is the important aspect of identification. One level on which the video works is by including us in part of the joke. The positioning of the static cameras, the dialogue, the need to resolve the enigma, the desire to know the outcome all combined to make us in some way part of what is going on. The video is cleverly constructed to make us identify with the action that is taking place.

Do you know a famous film that features the Mini? Do you think the producers of the video had this in mind when they made it? If you don't know, look here: www.youtube.com/ watch?v=RtWkewqIFDM.

Activity

How many of these ideas did you get yourself when you viewed the product? If you got all of them, well done. If you did not get them all, think hard about the ones that you missed out. Was this because you didn't fully understand what was going on? Or perhaps it dealt with a concept that you are unclear about. Make a careful review of what you did well and what you did not manage so well and use this as a guide to what you need to revise in readiness for the exam. You should try repeating this process for each of the four questions.

Question 2: Media Institutions – brand promoted

There are clear links here to question 1. The ability of the video to attract an audience is obviously important in terms of the promotion of the brand. You need therefore to focus on the question and try to avoid simply repeating question 1 material in this different context.

Note first that we are being shown an exciting video which is about speed (on the motorway) and about clever effects that show us daredevil stunts being performed by the Mini. (If you already knew about *The Italian Job* you will realise how the idea of performing stunts has been important for some time in terms of the Mini's brand image.)

Second, you might like to note that the context of YouTube and the idea of a viral video combined to make the Mini modern and trendy and that this is an important element of the creation of the Mini brand image. Similarly the association with a video game suggests that this is not some family saloon but a car which fun to drive, as illustrated by the way it is driven in the clip.

The witty dialogue and the 'blokey' patter on the soundtrack are also evidence of the way in which the brand is being promoted as a trendy product that people in the know will want to possess.

Finally think about the 'romance of the open road'. Owning a car, in this case a Mini, offers the audience the freedom to travel, to go where they please and, as in this instance, to take with them a travelling companion.

Question 3: Media Representations – real

For this question you are concerned with the representation of reality. So you are on the lookout for examples of how the product is made to appear as though it is real. There are a number of places you might start but it might be best to keep it simple by making some obvious choices. First, there is the way it is shot. As you will have noted in question 1, the camera positioned to look through the windscreen places the audience right inside the car with the driver and his passenger. This privileged view of the action also makes us privy to the sound that is important in the video. We have both diegetic sounds that you would expect to find if you were sitting inside the car, and the dialogue where you are listening to your fellow passenger commentating on the action taking place on the road ahead. You can focus on the dialogue and consider the chatty way in which they speak as a means of providing authenticity. Finally, there is the use of CGI, which offers a sophisticated simulation of the process of driving down a motorway. If you have done any work on postmodernism, you might also recognised that this playing with the idea of what is real and what is fake is one of the qualities to be associated with postmodern culture.

Question 4: Media Audiences – pass on message

This is quite a complex question and relies to some extent on your knowledge of social networking. However, bear in mind that it is the features evident in the video that you are primarily concerned with, so again be sure to start with the obvious. A basic appeal of the video is that the audience are put in the position of wondering whether what they are viewing is real or fake. This is a central enigma that hooks you into the video and makes you want to share it with others. The video is clever in other ways: the use of CGI and the witty banter between the characters can be cited as examples. The context of YouTube and the ease with which you can email or send a link to friends as well as embedding it on other sites all add to the appeal of sharing it. Finally, the fact that this video is not generally available other than via e-media can be said to encourage its appeal as a viral; people take pleasure in finding and sharing material that their friends may not yet have discovered.

Analysing a print product: the *i* newspaper

In January 2012, AQA set the front page of the *i* newspaper as the unseen product on which the Section A questions were based. The product was released in the form of an A3 insert in the exam paper itself and reproduced in full colour to closely resemble the actual front page of the newspaper. The front page story on this occasion was the sentencing of two young men to four years' imprisonment for inciting people to come to a riot via Facebook. The riot, however, never happened and many liberal-minded people felt the sentences were unnecessarily harsh.

Here is a summary of the information provided on the paper as background to this Section A product:

- *i* is seen as a new kind of newspaper.
- It appeals to all ages in its print form.
- It achieves interactivity via social networking sites.
- It is a reader-led newspaper for the twenty-first century appealing to people with limited time.
- The estimated 368,000 readership is mainly in the ABC1 group, people who work in professional and white collar jobs, with a high proportion of readers in the 15–24 age group.

You need to do two things. First, go to this site and get an update on the current readership figures for *i*: www.pressgazette.co.uk/story.asp?section code=1&storycode=49653&c=1. Second, go out to your local newsagent and buy a copy of *i*. If you forget or are too disorganised there is an example on p. 80, but it is better to have a full size copy in front of you.

NOTE

It is important to understand the meaning of figures given for newspaper distribution. Circulation refers to the number of copies actually bought by people whereas readership takes into account that for each copy bought a number of people may read it – for example, if it is delivered to a family home. Figures are further complicated by the fact that some copies are 'paid for' while other are given away free – for example, in hotels or on trains. A title such as *Metro* is free to anyone able to pick up a copy and if you have used public transport, you will see how many people pick up a 'used' copy and read it, thus increasing the readership.

Look carefully at the front page of your copy of *i*. If you want to have a go at the analysis under exam conditions, then you need to time yourself for the 15 minutes of reading time.

As with the DVD, read the questions first. The questions on the papers were focused as follows:

- Media Forms: Design of the front page to attract readers.
- Media Audiences: Appeal of the content to target readership.
- Media Representation: How news is represented as entertaining.
- Media Institutions: How is *i* branded as a new product in the age of online news?

The same advice for dealing with a print product is offered as that for a moving image. Divide a couple of sides of the space available for notes into the key concept headings.

Media Forms – attract readers

Let's have a look at the first question on the paper under the heading of Media Forms and explore how the front page of the newspaper is designed to attract readers.

Remember we need to note down the keywords, in this case 'attract readers'. As before under each of the headings we are looking for four or so points to make, with support from our scrutiny of the product to explain each one.

So, your notes might contain some of the following ideas:

- Design is clear and well-organised, giving the page a clean uncluttered appearance while still conveying a lot of information – e.g. the headline story is placed centrally to signal its importance in relation to the rest of the page.
- The page has a range of teasers inviting the reader to buy the newspaper and explore these teasers further on the inside pages. You need to find examples of these from the edition you have bought.
- The newspaper promises different items for different demographic groups within the target readership. Again look out for examples to support this idea.
- The feel of the newspaper is that it is very 'happening' and plugged in to current cultural vibes. The lower-case masthead and the prominent links to social networking sites give it a contemporary feel.

You might also refer to the appeal of its uniqueness – this is the only concise quality newspaper available.

Media Audiences – content appeal

The content and in consequence its appeal to target audiences will obviously change according to which day's copy of the *i* you have bought. However, it is likely that the type of content will remain fairly constant and that what will change will be the examples you need to use according to the edition that you have.

Remember that we have been told that the audience, although of all ages, is predominantly at the lower-end of the age demographic and that it is at the top end of social classification – mostly ABC1s.

The content, therefore, is represented as intelligent and informed while still being accessible. *i* readers are not patronised, so part of the appeal is the way in which the content is aimed at educated people capable of under-standing sophisticated ideas.

The content is broad in its appeal with items likely to appeal to younger and older people and to both genders as well as a wide range of tastes and interests.

> You might find it useful to look across a range of newspaper front pages for the day on which you bought the *i*. There are interesting comparisons to be made with the *Independent* itself as well as a more downmarket title such as the *Sun* or *Daily Star*.

Media Representations – news entertaining

Like all news media *i* focuses on people as a means of telling stories. This is evidenced through the number of photographs of people as well as the number of quotes of what people have said.

Headlines are used as a narrative enigma, the purpose of which is to hook the reader into going on and reading more of the stories in order to resolve the set enigma.

Similarly the teasers on the front page pose an enigma that can only be resolved by buying the paper and reading the inside pages.

Also the wide variety of news made available adds to the entertainment value. From hard news through to consumer articles and features, the *i* aims to provide something that will entertain each member of the readership.

Media Institutions – new kind

First, consider the format of *i*. What we have is a tabloid format, usually associated with more popular downmarket titles such as the *Sun* and the *Mirror*, but on this occasion offering serious and informed content of the type normally associated with the top end of the market.

The newspaper is portable and easy to handle and read while on public transport for example.

The design is user-friendly and appealing, making it easy to navigate and read.

The varied content provides an appeal to a broad audience while still ensuring appeal to the core target audience of young people.

Mark scheme

Mark schemes are published by AQA and other awarding bodies in the interests of transparency. They have probably been used by your teacher to help with the marking of your work and with understanding how you will be assessed in the exam. They are public documents which you are free to look at yourself. You can read the mark scheme for any of the past MEST1 Section A questions by visiting the AQA website. These tend to be made public about a year after the exam has been sat to restrict student access to material that teachers may wish to use for mock exams and other teaching purposes.

The function of a mark scheme is to help examiners arrive at a mark for each question on the exam. Examiners have to be trained for each series of the exam in how to interpret and apply the mark scheme to the responses that candidates produce. As well as descriptors which describe the types of response at different levels, examiners are also told what content to look out for when assessing what students have written.

The mark scheme for each question is divided into levels 4 down to 0. The marks for each level are as follows:

Level 4	10–12
Level 3	7–9
Level 2	4–6
Level 1	1–3
Level 0	0

Clearly to do well you will want your answer to be rewarded with marks in Level 4 if possible.

Here is the descriptor for level 4 for question 1 about Media Forms:

Thorough knowledge and understanding of the wide range of techniques used to engage the audience, demonstrated by detailed reference to the text and confident use of media terminology.

> NOTE
>
> It is important to remember that there are rarely any 'right' answers in a subject such as Media Studies. Examiners are guided as to the content they should look for in a student's response but equally they are told to be prepared to reward the unexpected. Some clever students come up with ideas that even the people who set the exam had not thought of.

Look at some of the keywords in the mark scheme. 'Thorough' implies detailed and well understood, so it is important to show that the knowledge and understanding you have is both of these things. 'Wide range of techniques' implies that there are a number of them (probably at least four and that they are different from each other, not the same point made in a different way). 'Detailed reference' means that you are producing a significant amount of evidence directly from the product. Confident use of media terminology means that you are using specialist subject vocabulary (words such as 'narrative', 'genre', 'close-up') which you have used and applied correctly.

So the mark scheme tells you a good answer should show:

- you know what you are talking about
- you can spot at least four different techniques being used to engage the audience
- you can support your ideas with evidence from the product you have watched
- you can write down your ideas using the appropriate terms you have learned in your Media Studies class.

> **NOTE**
>
> Media terminology. Many of the media products that are likely to be used for Section A analysis are intended for mass consumption. As such, the general public will probably be aware of them and also have a response to them. In some cases, members of the public may well have quite strong views and opinions about them. On this basis it could be argued that many people might feel equipped to have a go at Section A of MEST1. They would, however, most likely produce an informed layperson's response. That means that their response might appear quite coherent and convincing but would be lacking in important aspects that indicate that a student had followed a Media Studies course.

One important distinguishing feature of a response from a good Media Studies student is the ability to employ appropriate media terminology. If you want to get a good mark in this section of the paper, it is important to show that you not only know the important terms but can also use them correctly.

The terminology is basically of two types. First, what might be called a production vocabulary. These are terms that can be used to describe the features of a product in terms of how it has been produced. For example, with a moving image product you need to be able to use terms to describe the type of shot being used (e.g. close-up, long shot), camera movement (e.g. zoom, pan) and edits (e.g. cut, fade). Similarly you need to know the features for print product (e.g. headline, masthead, column, caption) and for websites (e.g. menu, hyperlink, embedded video). Many of these terms should become second nature to you through the work you have done on your MEST2 productions.

The second type of vocabulary you need is a more academic vocabulary and this you should have picked up through your work in preparing for MEST1 Section A and through your learning and reading during your Media Studies course. It is a good idea to remind yourself about some of the key terms under the headings suggested by each of the four key concepts (see below).

The key concepts

As is made clear in the specification, on the exam paper and in the mark scheme, the application of the key concepts is of prime importance to your success.

> Section A of MEST1 presents you with the challenging and demanding task of responding to four questions based on an 'unseen' product and can be drawn from a wide range of media output.
>
> Being adequately prepared to tackle these questions is absolutely essential if you are going to do a decent job on Section A. So what do you need to do to make sure you are adequately prepared?
>
> Well, you should be aware that the questions that you will be asked in Section A are based around four of the key concepts that should underpin your understanding of most of the study you have undertaken in the first year of your media course. These concepts should by now have become a familiar tool when you need to undertake any kind of analysis of media products.

NOTE

The key concepts can be listed as follows:

* Media Forms including Genre and Narrative
* Audience
* Representation
* Institution.

They will also form the headings for the four questions that you need to respond to in Section A but you may find that in the exam you take the order they are placed in is different.

This is a useful place to give you a quick reminder of what each of those key concepts is about and why they are so important, not just as headings for MEST1 Section A responses but also for all the other units covered by this book. Remember the key concepts are central to nearly all the work you do at AS and a good deal of it at A2.

Media Language (Media Forms)

Media Language
Media Language refers to the ways in which a media product is constructed – for example, by combining visual images, sounds and text.

Media Forms is primarily about the way in which products are constructed. When media producers create a media product, they make a series of decisions about how the finished product will appear. If it is a moving image product, these decisions are likely to begin with the *mise en scène* or the material that goes on in front of the camera – for example, the location and the people appearing in the product. There are also decisions made about how the camera is used: the type and size of shot has to be considered as well as the extent to which the camera moves with the action or stays still with the action moving around it. Finally there is the post-production process: editing the product into a coherent sequence, choosing what to include and what to cut as well as the sequence in which the action will be revealed.

> **NOTE**
>
> Note how much you are likely to have learned from your own attempts at creating media products. In a way analysis is the reverse process of constructing a product; indeed you will sometimes hear it referred to as deconstruction. When you are engaged in production, think about the decisions you made to create your final product. Why did you choose to use that camera angle? Why did you divide your Web page in that way?

What your learning in your AS course will provide you with is a toolkit so that for any product that comes under your scrutiny, be it in the MEST1 exam or elsewhere, you should be equipped to understand and explain the process by which it has been created.

We have already mentioned the important tools available to you for use in Section A analysis and the ability to explain how a product has been shaped the way it has. Two other tools are particularly handy to use under the Media Forms heading:

genre
The means of categorising media output into groups of products with distinct similarities in common.

- *Genre*. You will have studied genre in some detail as part of your AS course. Genre means to place media products together in similar categories. What it also does is provide you with a way of looking at products

in terms of their similarities to and differences from other products.
So in our look at the front page of *i* (p. 51), we might note that while the
page has features which make it similar to the front of popular newspaper
which use the tabloid format, it is also different from them in both design
and content. It is these similarities and differences which allow us to
explore some of the crucial aspects of the way in which media products
are put together.

- *Narrative*. Don't imagine that narrative is simply another word for plot.
  As you will have learned, narrative is more broadly a mechanism for
  exploring the way in which a media product has been created in order
  to communicate information to use. Narrative is therefore a useful tool
  in looking at how a print product or a news bulletin uses techniques such
  as enigmas to tease us into wanting them to reveal more information to
  use – for example, through tempting us with information on the cover
  that can only be fully revealed if we look inside. The best way to use narrative is to see it as an organising principle designed to control the flow
  of information from a media product to its audience.

narrative
The way in which information is organised and revealed by a media product. Includes both fictional products such as television soaps and factual information such as newspaper articles.

Media Audiences

Media Audiences
Groups of people who consume media products including print and e-media output as well as television, radio and cinema.

A lot of AS students struggle with the concept of audiences. A common
complaint among media teachers is that students seem to the think that the
characters portrayed within a media product will reflect the audiences at
which that product is aimed. There may, of course, be a grain of truth in that
assumption but in general this is not necessarily the case. A show such as *X
Factor* is targeted at a family audience via its prime time Saturday evening
slot. Its success is that it attracts a huge audience across quite a wide demographic. The age of the contestants, presenters and judges is probably more
to do with their appeal to this wide demographic rather than the targeting
of a narrow audience segment. Indeed if the show did target a narrow
audience segment, it would be unlikely to maintain the popularity it has
achieved.

So what do you need to know in terms of the key concept that is Media
Audiences? Well, breaking down a complex topic such as Media Audiences
into a few basic ideas is far from easy. You would really do better to read
about and get yourself fully up to speed with some of the main issues that
surround audiences. Assuming you have left it a bit late to do that or that you
simply want a reminder of the key ideas in readiness for the exam, here is
an attempt to provide an overview:

- You need to take on board that there are different types of audiences.
  These may vary from family audiences tuned in to *X Factor* through to

niche audiences, such as people who listen to classical music on BBC Radio 3. A good starting point to try to understand the complex nature of audiences and their behaviour is to observe both your own and your close family's media consumption.

- That leads neatly to the second point. What do audiences do with the media? Try exploring the Uses and Gratifications theory which seeks to explain how audiences use media output and how they derive pleasure from it. Consider your own media consumption in terms of the uses and gratifications it offers you.

- Another issue you need to be aware of is media effects. Trying to measure, predict or explain the effects the media may have on audiences has been an ongoing focus for Media Studies for many years. It is not going to be one that you are likely to resolve in your MEST1 exam but you do at least need to be aware that it is an important aspect of audiences as a key concept. In terms of Section A, some attempt to understand how the product is likely to impact on an audience can offer a valuable insight into how the product 'works'. This is especially the case if the product has been designed to have a specific effect – for example, an advertisement or the trailer for an upcoming broadcast or film.

- Finally, audiences were once seen as passive. Then they were seen as active, making choices and using media output in ways that gave them pleasure. In this age of digital media, they are almost overwhelmed with opportunities to interact with media output. The idea of audience participation is now fundamental to a significant amount of media across all the platforms. Showing an awareness of how this interactivity impacts upon as well as shapes media products is an important aspect of demonstrating your knowledge and understanding of this key concept.

Media Representations

Media Representations
The processes by which media producers select and present information to an audience. Representations are important because they usually carry with them the values and ideology of the producers who create them.

The problem with representations as a key concept is that it tends to become over-simplified too readily. Too often it is associated merely with the idea of stereotyping with little insight into the analysis of media products beyond this basic idea. A good way to get a handle on representation is the rather old-fashioned approach of seeing it as the process of re-presentation. This idea contains within it the concept that the media takes something that exists in the outside world and re-presents or re-packages it for the audience to consume. That thing in the real world might include a news event, a love story, a football match or even people living together in the jungle forced to eat insects and other nasties. Because the media both selects what it chooses to show us and how it chooses to do so, this process of representation takes on the values of the producers who have determined how to re-present the event to us. One way in which representation becomes more significant in this ideological way is through repetition. If the values implicit in a representation are constantly repeated across different media, it becomes hard not to see them as being true or simply the way that things are – for example, women, youth, ethnicity. The danger of course of the media being permitted to create and reinforce representations in this way is the impact they have on the groups who are so represented. Ultimately they become stigmatised and marginalised by the negative representations they have attracted.

So what do you need to look out for in terms of Media Representations in Section A of MEST1? Here is a list of some of the basic ideas that underpin the concept. You should find it useful to help you get focused on responding to whatever question is set under this heading in the exam:

- *Accuracy of representation*. Clearly you need to consider whether the representation is intended to be accurate before exploring this route. Generally you will be looking at the relationship between the thing being represented (e.g. the life cycle of a woman in the John Lewis advertisement) and the way in which the product you are scrutinising goes about the process of representing it.

- *Values/ideology*. Closely allied to the above point is that important issue of the values or ideology which are loaded into the representation. A simple way of approaching this is to ask yourself: in whose interest is it that we see the world like this? Advertisers, for example, often represent what they are selling as in some way having the capacity to make us happier if we purchase whatever it is they are selling. Hence products in advertisements are often represented as being essential or desirable if we are to make up for the deficiencies in our lives as we live them at the moment.

- *Self-representation*. One of the impacts of the increasing popularity of social networking is the opportunity for people to represent themselves directly to the world, rather than their image being mediated through mainstream media. In consequence, celebrities from the world of entertainment can speak directly to their fans (e.g. through Twitter), presenting to them what they would argue is a more honest and accurate representation than they might expect to read in the popular press, for example.

- *Stereotypes*. We mentioned earlier that one problem is that students see representation as entirely concerned with stereotypes and little else. With luck you may have realised that this is not the case. However, stereotypes do play an important role in our understanding of this key concept. The media often uses stereotypes as a kind of shorthand method of showing us a person or group of people by focusing on one particular

ideology
This is a term used frequently in relation to the social and political function of the media. Ideology is a system of belief – for example, capitalism or democracy. It is often argued that the media play an important role in supporting and upholding the dominant ideology within a society.

personality trait. Old men, for example, are seen as grumpy. Clearly media producers gain from this the great advantage that they can simplify complex issues and present them quickly and easily. Of course the danger of stereotyping is that we classify people into a group and that means we can end up dismissing them as real people. So one question you can ask when you look at how people are represented in the product you are exploring is: how far are they portrayed as real and believable people and how far are they simply two-dimensional media constructs created for ease and simplicity?

Media Institutions

Media Institutions
Also known as media industries, the term 'institutions' refers to producers of media output and includes large organisations such as the BBC and News International in addition to individual producers creating websites.

The word 'institutions' in the context of Media Studies has fallen from favour of late. Academics prefer to talk about Media Industries. There is an important reason for this that is reflected in the changes that have taken place in media production in recent years. The word 'institution' carries with it connotations of a large organisation with strict protocols and work methods. An organisation such as the BBC is very much an 'institution' with its value system of commitment to public service broadcasting. Murdoch's News International is similarly an institution, although many would say with a rather different set of values from those cherished by the BBC. While a good deal of media output is still in the hands of these monolithic media organisations, the impact of the Web and the shift from analogue to digital has created a much more complex pattern of media production than that which existed ten years ago. There are huge numbers of media producers (and distributors) on YouTube but few of these people would see themselves as media institutions. Many are individuals taking the opportunities presented by cheap and easily accessible technology to create and distribute products to a global audience.

> **NOTE**
>
> One of the reasons that you are provided with a few paragraphs of information on the exam paper about the media product you are being asked to consider is to provide you with some information about the context in which the product was produced. This should offer you vital clues as to its intention and function in relation to the content and the target audience. An important reason for reading the information carefully.

In the June 2012 exam paper, for example, the product was an introduction to an episode of *The Simpsons* created by the graffiti artist Banksy.

So, given that the section on 'industry' is likely to maintain the heading 'Media Institutions' for a while yet, here are some suggestions for areas you might like to consider when approaching this key concept:

- First, bear in mind where the product has originated from, what its intention is, who the target audience is and how it has been distributed. Understanding the purpose and function of a media product as well as the audience at which it is targeted is an important first step to a fuller understanding of the product itself.
- The next important step is to understand the nature of the institution that created and distributed the product. There is often a significant difference in the nature of a product which has been created by a commercial producer from one that has been created by a publically funded organisation such as the BBC. Consider, for example, the difference in the production values of a programme such as *Strictly Come Dancing* and its ITV rival, *Dancing on Ice*. Similarly a product created by an individual using basic technology and distributed via YouTube will be significantly different from a big budget cinema production created in Hollywood. An important factor here is 'production values' or the level of sophistication that the product exhibits in terms of such things as its *mise en scène* and the technology employed to create it.
- You might also consider under this heading the increasingly complex relationship between producer and consumer. For many years media institutions were seen as a centrifugal force pushing a message to an audience that was ill-placed to do anything other than accept what was sent their way. Today audiences are much more active in the way in which they interact and much more in a position to make complex choices about what media they consume and how they use it. When you are asked to look at the issue of institutions, be aware of how the audience is able to impact through this interaction on the nature of what is produced. In all media platforms the relationship between media producer and media consumer has become much more complex than it was at the end of last century.
- Much media output is now global. More and more media products are aimed at and marketed to a global market. This again has impacted markedly on the nature of media production. Many media producers are global players with interests across different media platforms. Often this means that an individual product will exist and be distributed in different formats both across media platforms and across international boundaries. Producers need to ensure they respond to the technological demands of operating across these different platforms and in a global market.
- Finally, nearly all media institutions are subject to a degree of media regulation. You do not necessarily need a detailed knowledge of how

each individual industry is affected by regulation, but it is useful if you understand some of the ethical issues that are likely to have an impact on how media producers go about their task – for example, having some understanding of the fact that people's right to privacy has to be weighed against the rights of the media to invade that privacy in order to uncover and make public wrongdoing of various sorts. An awareness of this ethical issue can provide a valuable insight into the nature of media output, particularly in relation to news and current affairs coverage.

NOTE

For many students, Media Institutions presents the greatest difficulty as a key concept that they have to learn to apply. This is a problem not only in Section A of MEST1 but also throughout their Media Studies GCE course. Strangely an understanding of the issues that relate to this key concept forms a large part of most people's perception of the media. The changing nature of the media itself, brought about by the development of digital and Web-based technologies, has presented us with a whole new range of ethical debates which flare up with some degree of frequency in the media itself.

Activity

Can you recall a couple of ethical debates that surround the media currently?

For example, on 24 August 2012, the *Sun* newspaper published a special 'souvenir edition' featuring a photograph of Prince Harry, third in line to the throne, cavorting naked with a naked woman in a Las Vegas hotel room. The *Sun* was the only British paper to print the pictures which had been readily accessible via a number of websites on line. The British press had been requested by the Royal Family not to publish the photographs despite their wide circulation through online sources. The *Sun* argued that it was in the public interest that the photographs be made available to the British public. It argued that it was not making judgements about the prince's behaviour; it did in fact argue that it liked the prince.

Activity

Imagine that you have been set the front page of the *Sun* as a product for analysis in Section A of MEST1. Under each of the key concept headings, make a note of what you think are the most important points you think you might need to address in relation to the product.

The *Sun* explained that the palace's lawyers through the Press Complaints Commission (PCC) had warned newspapers not to publish the photographs, claiming they would invade Harry's privacy and breach the PCC code. The publication of the photographs led to subsequent complaints from members of the public to the PCC. The *Sun* defended its position on publishing the photographs by arguing that they had already been widely available and scrutinised by millions of people online and that to withhold their publication would be absurd. It argued that *Sun* readers had a right to see them.

But there is a clear public interest in publishing the Harry pictures, in order for the debate around them to be fully informed. The photos have potential implications for the prince's image representing Britain around the world. The *Sun* argued this in its editorial.

The managing editor of the *Sun*, David Dinsmore, addressed *Sun* readers via an online video explaining that the key issue was the freedom of the press and the right of *Sun* readers to see photographs already available to millions of people on the internet.

Activity

Do you think this is an issue about the freedom of the press or simply an opportunity to print salacious pictures designed to embarrass and compromise a celebrity figure?

Using the key concepts for revision

Think about using the above breakdown of the key concepts as an aid to your revision. It is not intended to be a guide for how to approach Section A in the exam; remember that you should always be sure to respond to the specific questions you are set in the exam which are likely to focus on the areas identified above or at least something similar.

Activity

Make a note of the key features of each of the key concepts as identified above. Now have a look at a media product, preferably something of the sort you might meet in the exam. With these key points in mind, note down quickly your responses to the product under each of the key concept headings. Repeat two or three times daily until you get to sit the exam.

Practising Section A analysis

We spent some time above working through examples of products that had been examined on past papers. You can go to the AQA website and check through some recent past papers to see what other products have been set as part of MEST1 Section A. Obviously there is likely to be some limitation on the type of product that can be set. This will be in terms of suitability – for example, it must be appropriate material to use in a public examination – and also time. Given that you have only 15 minutes to absorb and respond to a product and that in the case of a moving image product you will need to view it three times, there is a clear limitation of the size of the product that can be set. It is worth bearing this in mind when you are looking for examples of products that you can use to practise on. In the realms of moving image, advertisements across different platforms, such as television and the Web, are useful to practise with, as are film and television programme trailers. Similarly the front pages of magazines and newspapers, and similarly the homepages of websites, are all potentially good materials to rehearse your skills in Section A analysis.

Another area that you might possibly examine is music and other promotional videos. These tend to be short and self-contained as well as enjoying a distinct viral appeal, which raises interesting points that you might be asked to explore under the headings of audience and institution.

A further option is to look at extracts from longer moving image products, so be prepared to look at opening sequences from films and television programmes. These can be especially interesting as they tend to be products that are designed in such a way that they present a great deal of information about what is to follow and how the themes and narratives are likely to develop.

NOTE

In June 2010, AQA examiners set the title sequence from a programme which featured Peter Andre. The programme had been broadcast the previous year and was called *Peter Andre – Going it Alone*. This was the opening to a typical celebrity 'reality' television series which laid bare Peter's life after his split from fellow celebrity Katie Price, aka Jordan. The programme was broadcast on ITV2, a channel which had featured previous reality series about the couple's married life.

You can get a flavour of the programme by clicking on the link www.youtube.com/watch?v=ihVpjmVcKBM, which features a montage of the type of clips that students taking the exam saw in the opening sequence.

Here is an example of the type of film trailer that you might be asked to respond to as part of Section A: www.youtube.com/watch?v=NtOSznn GkY&feature=relmfu.

It features the comedy film *Ted*, released in cinemas in the UK on 1 August 2012. The film starred Mark Wahlberg in the role of John Bennett and Mila Kunis as his girlfriend Lori Collins whose romantic attachment was severely tried by the antics of a teddy bear who had grown up as John's best friend which he had wished to come alive when he was eight years old.

Made by Universal Pictures for a budget of $50million, the film grossed over $200million in its first six weeks of release in the US alone.

Directed by Seth MacFarlane, best known for the creation of the long-running animation series *Family Guy*, *Ted* hit the number one box office slot in the UK, beating *The Dark Knight Rises* into second place. The trailer for the film had received over a million and a quarter hits on YouTube within a month of its release in the UK.

Activity

Watch the trailer – three times if you wish to work under exam conditions – then have a go at these questions:

1   Media Forms: What narrative features are used in the trailer to encourage the audience to see the film?

   Prompts. Think about the function of trailers and how they are used in cinemas – for example, the creation of enigma, fostering audience expectations, the significance of genre and the development of hybrid genres, use of comedy to position the audience, narrative conflict and the need for resolution (e.g. fairy story beginning, rom-com and buddy movie genres intertwined, conflict between bear and girlfriend, the conflicts between the adult world and childhood). This use of comedy encourages the audience to be sympathetic to the main characters.

2   Media Audiences: In what ways do you think the behaviour of Ted is designed to shock a potential audience?

Prompts. Associations of teddy bears with childhood and innocence, the use of children's and adult language.

3   Media Representations: How are relationships represented in the clip?

Prompts. Consider the relationships between the boy and the bear, the bear and the family, John Bennett and his girlfriend, the adult John and Ted.

4   Media Institutions: What did the film distributor wish to achieve by marketing through the YouTube platform?

Prompts. Opportunity to reach the target demographic of young adults. Opportunity for viral promotion. Association of YouTube with comedy output. Ability of audience to interact with trailer and recommendation via word of mouth.

Examiners' reports

After each exam series, awarding bodies publish reports on the way in which candidates have responded to the exam they have just taken. While not exactly riveting reading, these reports are made public and do contain some useful items of information, largely intended to help teachers prepare students for future exams in the series. If you visit the AQA website, you can download a copy of the report for this unit, although the latest one you may be able to get access to is likely to be a year or so out of date. Your teacher, however, should be able to get access to the most recent and may be prepared to share it with you. Below we have produced a short breakdown of the typical points that have been made in recent examiners' reports. They are useful to you to in two ways:

1   They suggest how you might focus your responses to the questions in Section A to maximise your potential mark.
2   They suggest some of the pitfalls you need to avoid when you take the exam.

Teachers who read the examiners' reports will tell you that there is a tendency for the same points to re-occur over a period of time. Below is a list of some of the points that feature often in reports on MEST1 Section A.

* Students taking the exam need to read the questions carefully and answer them rather than using the key concepts' formulaic way and ignoring the actual questions set.
* Students must spend time looking at the questions before they view or look at the product to be analysed. That way they will focus on the questions and avoid the pitfall above.
* Good candidates use media terminology appropriately and well.
* Only use theory if it is appropriate and you understand it. Don't bolt it on just to show you have learned it.
* Where you can, offer a range of points and support these with evidence from the product.
* Don't just list 'ways' but develop and support them to show you understand.
* Make sure you understand the nature of institutions before you go into the exam. Students often produce weaker responses under the heading of this key concept.
* Remember that audiences are complex and often made up of disparate groups of people. Be specific about the relationship between the product and the audience being targeted.

MEST1 INVESTIGATING MEDIA SECTION B: THE CROSS-MEDIA CASE STUDY

Assessment at a glance: Section B

- Section B is based on your cross-media case study.
- It assesses your knowledge and understanding of contemporary media products, concepts and issues.
- Answer *one* essay question from a choice of *two*.
- Section B is worth 32 marks.
- You should spend approximately 45 minutes on planning and writing your essay in Section B.
- The answer booklet has five blank pages for your answer, plus a page for notes.
- Section B assesses AO2, which is the ability to apply knowledge and understanding when analysing media products and processes to show how meanings and responses are created.
- The questions are designed to assess candidates' ability to:

  - apply their knowledge and understanding of the products and processes in their chosen topic area across the range of media platforms
  - explore how meanings and responses are created.

- As indicated within each level, Quality of Written Communication is taken into account.

How to approach Section B: the cross-media case study

Moving on from Section A

Once you have completed Section A of the exam, you will move on to Section B where you will write an essay – a further chance to demonstrate your knowledge and understanding of a range of media products and issues.

Section B has some marked differences from Section A and therefore requires different skills and preparation.

Differences

- In Section B the assessment is based on one essay rather than four short answers.

- The essay is worth 32 marks; there are five blank pages in your answer booklet (plus a page for notes and planning).
- While the starting point for Section A is an 'unseen product' (and therefore may not be a product or even media form that you've studied), Section B is based on the work you have done throughout the year and in particular the cross-media case study which you have prepared.
- Section B should not contain any unpleasant surprises or difficulty for you – as long as you fully prepare and revise the case study.

Similarities

- Both Section A and B assess your knowledge and understanding of media concepts, contexts and issues.
- Both ask you to apply this knowledge and understanding when analysing media products and processes to show how meanings are created.
- Both sections require you to write clearly and concisely and to address the question, but this is clearly more of a challenge when considering the demands of essay writing.

Why an essay?

Essay writing is one of the most traditional forms of assessment. Students have been asked to write essays to demonstrate their knowledge of a subject since the earliest days of formal academic assessment. Essay writing is often seen as old-fashioned and elitist, with some people concerned that it really only tests people's ability to write an essay and not – for example – their understanding of media. For a relatively new subject such as Media Studies which focuses a great deal on new forms of communication, it probably seems particularly odd that nearly half of your AS exam should be based on an essay. Therefore it's a good idea to stop and consider what the reasons are for writing an essay (and in doing so to also consider what you need to do to write a successful one).

What is an essay?

This may seem an obvious question with an obvious answer, but thinking about the basic aim and structure of an essay should help you to prepare effectively for this section. An essay is an answer to a question in the form of continuous prose, made up of connected paragraphs, which should develop an argument and therefore provide evidence of your research into the subject area. The aim of setting an essay in an exam (as well as for homework or coursework etc.) is to test your ability to *discuss, evaluate, analyse, summarise* and *question*. If you are able to do all these things in relation to your cross-media case study, then it does suggest that you have a very good, in-depth understanding of that topic area – and perhaps the essay is the best way to demonstrate this.

Exam tip

Knowing that you have to answer an essay question and knowing that it is on your case study means that there could be a temptation to go into the exam with your answer prepared. Some advice – DON'T! One of the reasons that 'answering the question' is so important in an exam essay is that it differentiates between students: between those who really understand the media concepts and issues and can therefore use them to address whatever question is asked and those who have memorised their response in order to regurgitate it in the exam, whatever the question. All the prepared answer shows the examiner is that you have a good memory – unfortunately that isn't in the mark scheme.

We will come back to strategies for preparing for the exam essay later, but first it is important to make sure that your cross-media case study is prepared before thinking about how to structure your material into an essay form.

The cross-media case study: essentials checklist

Your cross-media case study *must*:

- Include a *wide range* of media products (e.g. film, websites, radio, TV programmes, newspapers etc.). The range of products should include media from contrasting institutions and with different audiences to allow you to discuss a broader range of media issues.
- Cover *three* media platforms: broadcasting, e-media and print.
- Be relevant to the contemporary media landscape and focus on *media* institutions.
- Be of interest to you and something you think is worth researching. (Hopefully!)

The cross-media case study must *not*:

- Be limited to one central product. For example, the study of one film, its poster and its trailer does not provide enough examples to be able to discuss contemporary media contexts. Even a fairly complex marketing campaign for a Hollywood blockbuster (e.g. *Prometheus*, *Dark Knight Rises*, etc.) is not enough on its own to fulfil the need for a *wide range* of products. Remember: this case study is something you should have worked on throughout the year – you need something to show for it!

* Focus on old examples (to be safe, keep within the last five years) because the case study should be discussing the state of the media today rather than providing a historical survey.
* Be on an industry other than media. Nike, the NHS, McDonalds, River Island etc. are not media industries (although they may have a connection to media products and marketing).

Beyond the specific guidelines a good cross-media study should also:

* Have a good balance between breadth (a range of media products linked across three media platforms) and textual detail.
* Provide contrast through reference to different types of products, institutions and audience.
* Explore the relationship between audience, product and institution.
* Demonstrate knowledge of contemporary media issues.

Exam tip

A successful cross-media case study is one which reflects the role of the media today through the discussion of a wide range of products and different institutions.

Revision tip

What can you do if you realise at this late stage that your case study does not fulfil the requirements laid out in the first set of bullet points? That it in fact ticks all the 'what not to do' bullet points? The first thing to say is that there's no point wasting time blaming people at this point (although some serious self-reflection – did you follow instructions, meet the deadlines, take on board feedback etc.? – might be called for once the exams are over). Instead you need to salvage what you can in order to prepare yourself for the exam.

It is worth putting in the effort at this point because a case study which doesn't conform to the requirements in terms of the range of examples and media platforms can only be awarded low-level marks.

Some suggestions:

- If you have only studied one film – and this is a common failing – choose a contrasting example (low budget rather than blockbuster, British rather than US, etc.) and study the official website, marketing campaign and any coverage in the press.
- Ask yourself the following questions: Who made it and why? Who was the audience and how did they respond? (You could look at fan forums, Twitter sites, etc.) Was it a box office and/or commercial success? What is typical or unusual about the film? What does it tell you about the kind of films being made today?
- You could take this model and apply it to other areas such as TV programmes, newspapers, media institutions.
- Remember though that this really is a last ditch rescue attempt – hopefully it won't be necessary!

Revision techniques: which do you use? Which do you think would be helpful?

Hopefully at this stage in your experience of being a student, you have a fairly clear idea of how you learn most effectively. You may have done a form of assessment which told you whether you are, for example, a visual or kinaesthetic learner. Or you may just be aware that you find certain techniques more efficient for taking in information than others – perhaps you hate making lists but love mind maps or vice versa.

It's a good idea to spend some time thinking about the range of revision techniques you use and how you use them. The list below may give you suggestions for some new approaches to use or remind you of some tried and tested techniques.

- **Index cards, mind maps and notes**

  - Use to record key points
  - Incorporate pictures, colour, highlighting

- **Learning posters and visual material**

  - Use pattern, colour, symbols and drawings

- Cover key points and topics
- Pin them up where you'll see them often

• **Key words, phrases, themes or concepts**

- Use your class notes, introductions, summaries, key questions to discover what's central in the cross-media study
- Use two or three sentences to define each central concept and add examples

• **Summary tables or grids**

- Compare or evaluate issues, debates, media forms

• **Teach someone**

- Teach a topic to a fellow student or a friend
- Thinking it through is effective revision
- Fill in the gaps in your knowledge as you identify them

• **Reinforce your memory**

- As you end a revision session, make a note of the key points covered
- Keep these and review again regularly.

(Adapted from Open University 'Skills for Study')

www.open.ac.uk/skillsfor study/index.php

Reviewing and organising your case study

The first step for effective revision is to feel organised and in control of your material. If you have lots of bits of paper in different files with seemingly little connection to each other, or to the exam, the process of revision can feel very daunting. Organising the key areas of your case study will help you check that it fulfils the requirements discussed above and provide a good foundation for the next stage of exam preparation. (For those students who already have beautifully organised notes, who have colour-coded, indexed and alphabetised the case study – you may want to miss out the next part and rejoin the rest of us later in this section.)

Step 1: constructing a content analysis and checklist

The following examples outline a possible approach to constructing a content analysis and checklist for your case study – you may wish to use your own techniques. The first, using a summary table, is based on a news case study.

Table 2 *What media products have I studied?*

Media platform 1: print	*Media platform 2: e-media*	*Media platform 3: broadcasting*
Front pages: the *Sun*, the *Mirror*, *Daily Telegraph*	Website analysis: guardian.co.uk, Mail online, BBC News	BBC News at 10/ITV News at 10 Local news broadcasts
Whole paper analysis: *i*	Range of apps produced by news organisations	Rolling news: Sky/BBC
Local paper coverage of particular story		

Figure 1

Sport case study mind maps.

The second example, using a mind map, is based on a sport case study.

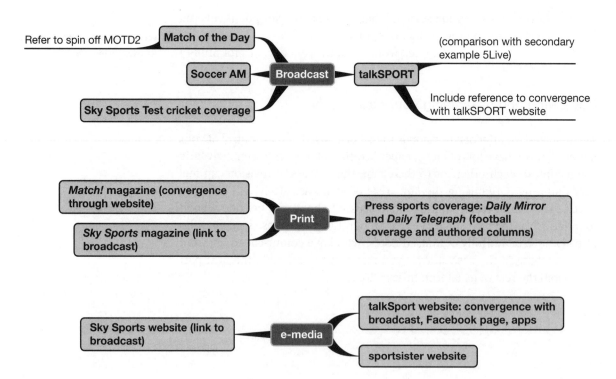

Once you've listed the content of your case study you should feel confident that you've covered the requirements of a wide range of media products covering three media platforms. There may initially seem a lot of material to cover in your revision but the case study should represent almost 50% of your AS study.

Activity

With the content of your case study fresh in your mind, review what you already know about the topic area. You could test this by thinking about how you would explain to a friend what you have discovered during your study of the news. This should just be a brief summary at this point – try to come up with about three key points. Below are some prompts to help.

For a news case study:

- What have been the major technological changes in how news is delivered and consumed in the last ten years?
- What are the dominant conventions of broadcast news?
- Is there a future for print-based news?

For a sport case study:

- Which sports and sports broadcasters are dominant in the UK?
- Who are the most important audiences for sports broadcasters?
- How has new technology affected the way audiences access sports coverage?

The aim of isolating a few key points from your case study is to illustrate your existing conceptual knowledge of the area which has been reinforced over the year of AS study. Revision should really be about reminding yourself of the detailed examples you will use in the exam to give evidence for your argument. If you found it difficult to come up with some key points then don't panic. Come back to this activity once you've done some detailed revision – you probably just need some more reminders.

Exam tip

You won't have time to include all the areas you have studied in your exam answer – but the more examples you have to choose from, the more flexibility you have to select the most relevant ones.

Step 2a: what range of products, institutions and audiences does my case study contain? News

Identifying the different types of media contained in your case study will develop your revision in more detail, help you to think about the different contemporary media issues which are likely to be relevant to the exam and provide a final check that your case study is as diverse as it should be. The following example uses the news case study again, first through a simple checklist and then by writing the findings up into continuous prose. The checklist headings provide a template for any case study – although you way need to modify it slightly – and suggests the variety of styles and contexts expected.

Table 3 News case study checklist

Institutions	Media products and audiences
Public Service Broadcasting: BBC News and website	Mainstream mass audience appeal: ITV news, tabloid newspapers, Sky News
Commercial: ITV (with PSB remit) *Daily Mail*, the *Sun*, *Daily Mirror*	Niche audience: local news, news apps
Global, multimedia conglomerates: Sky	Alternative/independent news products: no products studied in this context – might this be an area to address?
Trust: The *Guardian*	Mode of address: diverse range of styles from the *Telegraph* to the *Sun* to *i*, BBC and Sky News
	New technology: development in online news sources, effects on traditional news gathering, publishing and broadcasting

Summarising the list of examples from your cross-media study should help you to see any weak areas which you will need to address. The process of writing up your findings is also another way of reinforcing your knowledge.

SUMMARY OF CHECKLIST

The news cross-media study clearly has a wide range of institutions, products and audiences. The inclusion of products from Sky and the BBC provides the opportunity to analyse contrasting institutional contexts, the different ways in which the organisations are run and how this affects (if it does) the types of news produced. This context would be relevant in discussing one of the key debates in contemporary news media – what is the future of the traditional news products such as TV bulletins and newspapers in the age of online news? While there are clear differences, it is also important to look at similarities between commercial and public service institutions: the BBC has a similar strategy of synergy as Sky. In the newspaper industry, the changing role of the traditional tycoon owner is seen clearly with Alexander Lebdev, the owner of *i*, the *Independent* and the *Evening Standard* – a Russian businessman often referred to as an oligarch. It may be that it is only a few

Figure 3
Front page of the *i* newspaper.

incredibly wealthy individuals who are able to support a declining newspaper industry.

The choice of media products provides a diverse range of forms and styles, particularly across news websites and the print media. An obvious contrast in mode of address would be between an example of the popular press (the *Sun*, *Daily Mirror*, etc.) and a broadsheet (*Daily Telegraph*) as this would provide examples of how style and content are linked to target audience. The range of newspapers – and websites – means that this could be analysed across gender, age, lifestyle and politics rather than the more narrow and restrictive focus on class. The breadth of print products also provides detailed examples of how the industry has responded to declining sales in different ways (*i* and *Daily Telegraph*), analysing how they've attempted to attract new and different audiences.

The inclusion of a local newspaper and a regional news bulletin does provide some more variety in terms of news values and target audience. Regional news provision is also an area which has undergone huge changes in recent years and is under threat due to declining readership and therefore makes it a useful contemporary media debate. The one area that is lacking in the case study is any example of independent or alternative news media – all the examples are really the products of dominant, commercial institutions. Although there is plenty of diversity in the case study for it to be successful, having noticed this omission it is probably worth looking for some examples of alternative news organisations.

Step 2b: what range of products, institutions and audiences does my case study contain? Lifestyle

Table 4 *Lifestyle case study checklist*

Institutions	Products and audiences
Public Service Broadcasting: BBC terrestrial channels, website	Mainstream, mid-market, mass audience appeal, primarily female: *Great British Bake Off*, *Hairy Dieters* (and websites)
Public service/commercially funded: Channel 4 and More4	Niche audience, young, female: *Asian Lifestyle* magazine, handbag.com
Private, commercial corporations: Hearst Corporation (*Men's Health*, handbag.com), Sublime Global media (*Asian Lifestyle Magazine*)	Female, ABC1 target, rebranding (More4): *Kirstie's Handmade Britain*, *Fabulous Baker Boys*, *Gok Cooks Chinese*, *Grand Designs*, etc. (and websites) Male audience: *Men's Health* magazine and website

Schnews (www.schnews.org.uk/index.php) is a direct action news organisation run by volunteers. *Schnews* started as a free sheet but now has an extensive website which utilises a lot of the new technology and social networking techniques of the mainstream media.

Media Lens (www.medialens.org/) was set up to counter what it sees as the propaganda and misinformation provided by corporate press organisations and therefore provides a completely different perspective on news stories and also attempts to cover stories which are ignored by the mainstream press.

Indymedia Uk (www.indymedia.org.uk/en/) is part of a global organisation of 'DIY' news production which also provides links to a range of other alternative news websites (interestingly the website states that it is currently formulating a policy for use of Twitter and will not use Facebook).

Figure 4
BBC food programme
homepage

SUMMARY OF CHECKLIST

The lifestyle case study provides a good range of institutions which can be used to discuss several contemporary media issues including models of public service broadcasting, multi-platform corporations and the effect of digital technology on traditional media. The emphasis is on British broadcasting institutions but the inclusion of Hearst Corporation (US) and Sublime Global Media (India) gives some points of contrast. More4 makes a particularly good institutional case study as it is part of the Channel 4 group of channels – this provides the opportunity to analyse the structure of a contemporary media business with its use of new technology, a range of media platforms and channels which target a specific range of audiences.

More4 itself has been recently relaunched and rebranded with a renewed focus on lifestyle programming and a move away from the documentaries and arts programming which was previously part of its schedule. This development will be excellent for discussing the different ways in which media institutions are attempting to attract new audiences. Lifestyle is also a key part of the BBC's strategy to attract a mass prime time audience while also serving its public service remit. Programmes such as *The Great British Bake Off* and *The Hairy Dieters* are promoted through an educational context (teaching traditional baking skills, living a healthy lifestyle) as well as an entertainment one. This is also apparent in the BBC lifestyle websites, which provide links to guidance on healthy eating.

There are probably more similarities than differences in terms of the styles and target audiences of the lifestyle TV programmes in the case study, which isn't that surprising. For example, both the BBC and More4 programmes are aimed at mass audiences, all are built around a personality or star of the show and there seems to be a trend for the promotion of a traditional lifestyle brand, perhaps linked to the fashion for vintage clothes and furniture of recent years. This would provide an opportunity for analysis of the *mise en scène* of, for example, the images used on *The Great British Bake Off* and *Kirstie's Homemade Britain* to discuss target audience as well as values and ideology. There is some room to discuss a range of audiences through *Men's Health* and *Asian Lifestyle Magazine* as well as the young female audience for handbag.com. Again the rebranding of More4 is useful as it attempts to attract the female, 30–40 age range from an ABC1 demographic. This strategy is explicit when comparing the More4 lifestyle products with the BBC's more mass appeal ones. The More4 lifestyle website, recently redesigned as a 'scrapbook', is similar to Pinterest, the social bookmarking site which attracts a similar audience.

The connection to Pinterest also suggests a way of introducing the development in lifestyle genres created by new technology which would be useful for a question about the changing relationship between audiences and institutions. Similarly the inclusion of *Men's Health* magazine and website provides a case study for examining the future of traditional print magazines within the context of declining sales. The launch of a new magazine (*Asian Lifestyle*) demonstrates that there is still potential for print sales but using a new model of distribution.

Exam tip

Don't forget the print platform! It is common in exam answers for the print platform to be either dealt with very briefly or forgotten about completely and this has major implications for the level you can be awarded. Although you don't need to refer to all the platforms equally, you do need to show that you've used examples from all three. Often the problem is that the print does feel like an add-on in your cross-media study – a poster or review for example – rather than the main focus. Therefore it is important that you have at least one example where the main media product is the print platform. The other reason for the sidelining of print is the feeling that it's a traditional media in a state of decline in a digital world and is therefore less relevant. While sales of newspapers and magazines are certainly in decline, they still sell millions of copies to a range of audiences which provides a wealth of material for this kind of study. In addition the strategies used to try and address the decline in print sales would make a great media issue to analyse.

Step 3: linking the products to the concepts and issues

One of the key requirements of Section B is that you not only *answer the question* by making *detailed reference* to your cross-media study but also link those examples to *key concepts and issues*. This is clearly a challenging task, but there are certain approaches and techniques which will make it much easier. The first is to thoroughly revise the connections between your products and the key concepts so that you can easily access them in the pressurised exam context, rather than having to start from scratch wondering which example would be good to discuss audience, representation, institution, etc.

Media Issues

For this key concept it is particularly important to demonstrate your understanding of specialist terminology. The following are a few reminders of terms that sometimes cause problems.

convergence

This is an attempt by institutions to gain profit by making a range of media companies and technologies work together.

The ideal model in convergence would be for the consumer (audience member) to be able to use one piece of technology (e.g. a tablet, smartphone, internet TV, X-Box) for all their media needs (e.g. watching E4 or YouTube, posting on Facebook, listening to radio programmes, downloading or streaming music and films, Skyping, emailing).

The media concepts

The specification identifies the following areas which need to be included in your case study:

* *Audience*. How audiences receive, respond to and create products. This will cover a whole range of different target audiences and modes of address as well as user-generated content. You will also need to consider how new technology has created new ways for audiences to consume, comment on and affect media products.
* Remember: don't make the assumption that new technology always means that audiences are active and more powerful than for traditional media, think carefully about whether increased options for consuming media really mean more choice for the audience.
* *Institutional contexts*. How does the nature of the institution (independent, commercial, public, etc) affect the content of products and the way in which they are produced?
* Remember: make sure you can name the institution or company which produced each of your examples. If your product is from a commercial institution, try to think whether a public company would have produced the same piece of media (and vice versa). If not, why not?
* *Representations*. How are these constructed and understood?
* Remember: in analysing how a representation is constructed, you will need to use some detailed analysis and then link this to the relevant audience and institution.
* *Codes and conventions*. Identification of semiotic, generic and narrative conventions within individual products and across topic areas. What is similar and different about them?

- Remember: focus on the key areas which make your media products either unusual or common – select carefully in the exam, you don't want to waste time listing all the generic and narrative conventions when only a few examples are likely to be relevant.
- *Features and issues*. For example, synergy, convergence, intertextuality, cross-media promotion, public service remits, regulation, new technologies.
- Remember: some of these issues will be more or less relevant to your specific case study so don't panic if you haven't covered them all. Keeping up to date with developments in the media is really important to address this area – see the section on media resources (p. 221) for advice on this.

LINKING USING MIND MAPS

One way to revise linking products to concepts and issues is through the use of a mind map. This allows you to take a product from your case study and identify all the different ways you can use it to discuss the concepts. Staying with the example of news, this mind map takes one of the products studied and links it to the key media concepts.

On reviewing the mind map it is clear that some of the concepts are more relevant – there is more to write about them – than others. With the website example the concept of institution seems to be the most relevant and so that would structure the next stage of your revision.

synergy
A media strategy particularly associated with global multimedia conglomerates, where a single concept (e.g. a film, a musician, a franchise) is sold (or as it is sometimes referred to, 'exploited') across a range of different media but which are all owned by the same institution. Synergy has most explicitly been developed in the film industry where film studios, as part of a larger conglomerate, are able to develop marketing campaigns and merchandising across a range of media. It is important to question the success of the synergy strategy – does it work for all media? What effect has it had on the type of media products which are produced? etc. – and to consider how it has been affected by convergence.

Figure 5
BBC News website mind map.

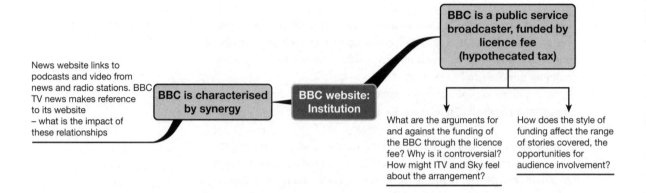

News website links to podcasts and video from news and radio stations. BBC TV news makes reference to its website – what is the impact of these relationships

BBC is characterised by synergy

BBC website: Institution

BBC is a public service broadcaster, funded by licence fee (hypothecated tax)

What are the arguments for and against the funding of the BBC through the licence fee? Why is it controversial? How might ITV and Sky feel about the arrangement?

How does the style of funding affect the range of stories covered, the opportunities for audience involvement?

Figure 6
BBC website institution mind map.

intertextuality
A concept associated with the emergence of postmodernism in the 1980s but that is now a mainstream style. Intertextuality refers to the way in which one media product can contain references to a range of existing products. This may be in the form of a remake or a sequel or through the copying of particular styles, dialogue, sound track, etc. Intertextuality is particularly apparent in films, TV and music videos. For the audience, intertextuality can provide pleasure, making us feel special for recognising specific references and creating a connection with the product and other people who consume it.

Activity

This stage of revision where you focus on one product and concept begins to raise the wider aspect of media issues.

• Which issues raised in the mind map above relate to the news and the BBC as an institution?
• Now take your own example from your case study, apply the media concepts and then choose one to focus on in more detail.

Step 4: linking concepts and debates to products

The most straightforward approach to revising the cross-media study is to start with your group of products and work out from that, moving from the micro (the product) to the macro (the concepts and issues).

A way of further testing your understanding through a different – and perhaps more complex – approach would be to reverse this process, i.e. to start with the media concept and issue and demonstrate how these link to your chosen products. The following gives an example of this by starting with the institution – in this case Sky – and linking it to the products studied:

Institution: multimedia, global conglomerate: News Corporation, owner of News International and Sky broadcasting.
 Can the *Sun* and Sky News be seen as characteristic products of a conglomerate?

Consider:

* cross-media promotion
* profit motive
* market share/audience.

What media issues are relevant in considering the role of conglomerates in the media today?

* The economic power of News Corporation has meant that newspapers such as the *Sun* and *The Times* are still being published despite the industry being in decline.
* Sky News, with its rolling, 24-hour broadcasts and hi-tech presentation, created competition for terrestrial news programmes which had to update the way in which they presented the news.
* Conglomerates such as News Corporation have been at the forefront of integrating new technology which has changed the way we consume media.
* Some suggestions: global dominance of a few media conglomerates may restrict choice and diversity; powerful institutions such as News Corporation believe they face unfair competition from public service broadcasting which could affect the funding of the BBC.
* Due to its position as part of a huge conglomerate, Sky is able to buy up programming (sports broadcasting, US drama series, etc.) which had previously been free to air.

Activity

Take each of the media concepts and apply the following questions to your case study:

1. Institution

    * What type of institution (PSB, independent, commercial, national, global conglomerate, etc.)?
    * Give details of the specific institution (name, key characteristics).
    * Which products have you studied belong to the institution?
    * What is there about the products which is typical of the institution?

2. Audience

    •   What different types of audience behaviour are associated with your case study?
    •   What theories of audience have you studied and how can these be applied to your products (these might include uses and gratifications, active audience, etc.)?
    •   What different types of mode address are apparent across products?

3. Representation

    •   Consider the key issues around representation (e.g. marginalisation and/or dominance of particular groups and/or places; possibility of self-representation, etc.)
    •   How could the products you've studied be used to discuss these issues?

Using both the product first and concept first approaches should mean that you build up a thorough, confident understanding of your case study and the issues it raises. This will provide an excellent foundation to answering whatever question you're given in the exam.

Exam tip

Section A of the exam is explicitly based on analysis and making detailed reference to the unseen product. Section B is different as the essay focus is on the wider media concepts such as audience and institution. However, it is very important that you don't lose focus of the product itself, whether it's a newspaper, TV programme or website.

One of the tricky aspects of Section B is how to keep the balance between reference to the wider concepts and discussion of your products; it is important that you don't end up making very generalised, descriptive references to the cross-media case study products.

Once again this really needs some pre-planning and you should start by asking yourself what kind of textual references will be relevant.

PREPARING FOR THE EXAM: REFERENCE TO PRODUCTS

To be fully prepared for Section B you do need to have a thorough knowledge of your products and how they are constructed. The difficult part is that you need to select which aspects of this construction are relevant to the question. You must avoid simply reproducing a piece of detailed analysis – no matter how accomplished – of, for example, a film sequence. Instead the analysis must be linked to the concepts and debates. Your aim is to demonstrate your familiarity with the product (in writing about the case study it is very easy to become general and descriptive) but without veering off into irrelevant detail.

Activity

For each media concept think about how reference to the product will be most relevant – remember, not every product will be appropriate for every concept. Use the following example as a model for your own choice of product. This time the example is a music video from a case study on the music industry.

Step 5: linking analysis to media concepts

The following analysis is in response to the past paper question:

'All media texts tell stories'. In what ways is narrative used in the media products in your case study?
    In your answer you should:

- provide a brief outline of your case study
- discuss the different ways narrative functions in the media products in your case study
- support your answer with reference to a range of examples from *three* media platforms.

The instruction to give examples of '*what ways is narrative used*' means that you will need to demonstrate exactly how narrative functions in the media products of your case study; this can only be achieved through detailed reference to the product.

SAMPLE ANALYSIS

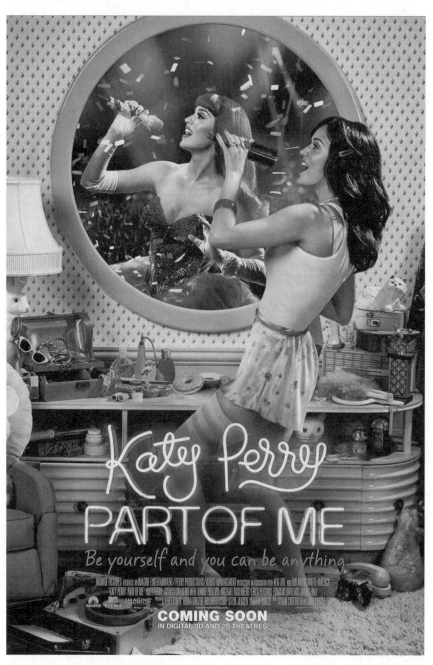

Figure 7
Katy Perry *Part of Me* film
poster.

Last Friday Night is a narrative rather than a performance music video. It is conventional of this style of video in that the artist – Katy Perry – takes on a role and acts out a storyline which has a direct relationship to the lyrics of the song. The construction of the narrative uses enigma and flashback to introduce and develop the story of 'last Friday night'. The video opens by referencing the conventional narrative techniques of a teen movie or TV series with an establishing shot of a typical American suburb, before introducing the central character Kathy Beth Terry, played by Katy Perry. Kathy is in her bedroom, having just woken up, and the narrative is constructed from her point of view so that the audience is positioned with her.

The music video uses intertextuality throughout; the references to popular culture are part of the mode of address and reinforce the nature of the target audience: female, in their early teens. Most explicitly the narrative of *Last Friday Night* refers to John Hughes films such as *Pretty in Pink* and *16 Candles*, teen movies from the 1980s which have been rediscovered by a younger audience through their availability on YouTube, iTunes and Netflix, etc. The narrative of these films focuses on the character of an outsider who is transformed into a beautiful young woman, a plot which is also recognisable from fairy tales, and it is this conventional narrative which structures *Last Friday Night*. Various cameo appearances by actors from *Glee*, young pop stars such as Hanson as well as 1980s child stars (Debbie Gibson and Corey Feldman) also work to construct a narrative world which is specific and recognisable to the target audience.

The narrative of *Last Friday Night* is used to address a young female audience who are Katy Perry's core fans. The plot line of the video is carefully constructed to appeal to this specific audience in a variety of ways. The star persona constructed by Katy Perry is aspirational but also attainable; the narrative context of the video works to display that persona. 'Kathy' is seen in two stereotypical gender representations – the geek who wears braces and child-like boyish clothes, while in the transformation scenes she is the popular girl who is stunning, fashionable and sexual. This fantasy of transformation, of being revealed, recognised and envied is a representation which is repeated throughout popular culture aimed at young women in magazines, TV series, films and advertising. These kinds of representations are criticised in a feminist analysis which argues that the function of these types of narrative is to train young women to value appearance and the importance of attracting a man over other achievements.

The narrative of *Last Friday Night* is also an important part of the Katy Perry brand, which builds on the romantic fantasy aimed at teenage girls through the album *Teenage Dreams* and the recent documentary about the singer, *Part of Me*. In this context the function of the video narrative is to provide pleasure for the viewer while watching the video itself but also to make the viewer want to prolong the experience by purchasing the single, the album and by going to see the film starring Katy Perry. In this way the narrative is part of a carefully constructed marketing campaign which promotes and sells the Katy Perry brand.

Activity

Read the analysis of *Last Friday Night* and make a note of:

- any references to specialist media terminology
- references to narrative codes and conventions
- how the analysis addresses the question
- references to critical approaches and media issues.

Now take an example from your own case study and write a paragraph which analyses the different ways narrative is used.

A SUCCESSFUL CASE STUDY: MUSIC

If your case study is on music, it's important to make sure that you include a range of different artists and groups who have different audiences and are connected to different institutions. If Katy Perry was part of the case study, then you would need a good contrasting example who appeals to a completely different demographic. If one of your artists is a mainstream artist backed by a global institution, then it would also be good to compare them with a more independent or niche artist. Remember – the starting point doesn't have to be an artist, it could be a magazine or TV channel.

SUGGESTED CONTENT: MUSIC CASE STUDY

Katy Perry (music video, Twitter, Facebook, album covers, merchandising, documentary film, film poster)
Institutions: Capitol Records (Sony), MTV films
Audience: mass market, young female demographic, mainstream, commercial

A contrasting artist in terms of audience, institution and mode of address, some suggestions: James Blake, Lykke Li, M.I.A.

NME (print and online magazine, TV channels, Twitter, Facebook)
Institutions: IPC – TimeWarner

Audience: niche, middle aged, male; popular artists: Radiohead, Arctic
Monkeys etc.

Exam tip

Exam questions with specific reference to institutions are – not surprisingly –
a common feature of Section B. When students answer an institution question
through a music case study there is often some confusion with music artists
being referred to as if they are institutions in themselves.

It is important to make sure that you study the institutions of the music
industry, just as you would if you were studying Hollywood, say – and think
about how the nature of the industry affects the output of the artists.

Some music institutions: Virgin, EMI, Universal, Island, Warner Bros
(remember – the institution behind your chosen artist is very likely to be part
of a global conglomerate).

Useful link: the *Guardian's* site on the business of the music industry covers
a range of recent stories which would be relevant to discussing the role of institutions in the music industry: www.guardian.co.uk/business/musicindustry.

Step 6: approaches to writing about institutions – getting the balance right

In the previous example, looking at the use of textual detail in an exam essay,
the aim was to foreground the construction of a media product to be able to
analyse the use of narrative. In contrast to this, if you have a question which
foregrounds institutions (or audience), you need to shift the emphasis while
still demonstrating your familiarity with media products. Remember, the
important thing is to make clear to the examiner that you have spent time
studying and analysing your examples, and that you haven't just read about
them on the internet.

The following example uses a film cross-media study to address a
question on institutions:

> Synergy is the process by which media institutions use a range of
> platforms to promote, sell and distribute their products. Assess the
> impact of synergy in your cross-media study.

The instruction to '*Assess the impact of synergy*' means that you must not just
describe the ways in which synergy has been used, but also evaluate it.

Exam tip

When using the marketing of a Hollywood blockbuster as part of a case study, it is important to be selective in your references. You don't need to list every piece of promotion and merchandise that was used, just the ones which are relevant to the question. Although it's tempting to include everything you know, it can be counterproductive as it doesn't demonstrate understanding of the question and can become a rather tedious list for the examiner to get through.

Synergy is now used routinely by media institutions to promote, sell and distribute media products. This is particularly true of the film industry where synergy was identified as a way of dominating the marketplace in the late 1980s. Two of the institutions in my film case study are typical of this development: Disney and Fox studios are both part of global multi-media conglomerates which means that they are ideally situated to promote their latest releases through the use of synergy. In both the examples I looked at – the distribution of *Tron Legacy* and *Prometheus* – the institution was using synergy to market a film sequel where the aim was to attract a new audience, along with the audience which remembered the earlier instalment in the franchise. In assessing the impact of synergy on the films and their institutions it can be argued that while Disney was able to use a variety of platforms to target different audiences, Fox's very elaborate synergy campaign was less successful in moving out from the core audience.

Activity

Read through this introduction again and this time note down the information you've been given.

*   What is the cross-media study? Does it cover a range of examples?
*   What specialist media terminology is used? Are you familiar with all the terms? If not look them up.
*   How does this introduction answer the question? What does it say has been the impact of synergy on the cross-media study?
*   Do you think this is a successful opening to an exam essay? Does it make you want to read on?

Tron: Legacy is a 'tent pole' movie which must appeal to a wide audience rather than the cult audience of the first film in 1982. There was a great deal of interest in the sequel but this was really only amongst a niche audience: those who remembered the original (now in their late thirties and early forties which is outside Hollywood's target market), fan boys, geeks and sci-fi fans. *Tron: Legacy* had an estimated budget of $170m, and to be financially successful it had to 'open up' to a much wider, more mainstream audience, but without losing the cult status which would attract the core audience. To do this Disney employed synergy, matching the media platforms to the target audience – something which Disney as a conglomerate is able to do.

To target the core fans, Disney used traditional media products such as trailers (released at ComicCon) but also online games and apps as well as engaging with fan forums and bloggers. As is typical during the build-up to the release of this type of film, Disney controlled the 'leaking' of information to bloggers and Twitter users in order to heighten expectation. Disney was able to assess the impact of the synergy strategy by monitoring the interaction with users; the online game was seen as particularly successful with 4.5 million registered players. However, these users were always going to be predominantly young, male and interested in technology. For *Tron: Legacy* (and any intended blockbuster) to be a genuine hit it also needed to appeal to the audience beyond this, to groups defined by Disney's marketing team as mothers, children and non-technophiles. It is this ability to market a film to a range of audiences which demonstrates the value of synergy to institutions. Disney addressed the mainstream, family audience through features in its theme parks (both in the US and Europe), the launch of an animated mini-series on its cable channel and new posters and trailers. As well as using different media platforms from those used for the core audience, Disney also shifted the focus of the marketing, emphasising the father-son relationship and emotionally satisfying narrative over the sci-fi genre and new technology.

Activity

Re-read the two previous paragraphs.

- What argument is given for why an institution needs to use synergy?
- What examples are referred to?
- What media concepts are discussed?

A problematic feature of this analysis so far is that there is almost no evidence of detailed engagement with the media products within the cross-media study. Looking at the paragraphs above it is clear that these examples could be cited without the student ever having seen a poster or trailer for the film or having played the online game. To try to address this – but without moving away from the question focus, the next section analyses one of the products in greater detail.

The use of synergy is clearly central to the marketing of Hollywood blockbusters but it is also worth noting that one of the most traditional forms of film distribution – the trailer – has remained one of the most important. In this context, synergy is effective in delivering the different trailers to different audiences much more effectively than before the move into multiple platforms. The first teaser trailer, which was revealed at ComicCon but was then posted on YouTube, fan forums and played at the end of the online games, directly addresses the core audience. It is virtually indistinguishable from a video game in style through the use of computer-generated imagery and its narrative: the trailer starts in the middle of a chase between two futuristic bikers against a neon back drop; there is no information about character or story line. The only line of dialogue, 'You won . . . this is just a game', is also an allusion to gaming. The *mise en scène* and electronic soundtrack reinforces the sci-fi genre which will also appeal to the target audience. A later trailer distributed on more traditional platforms – cinema, TV – is very different. The later trailer is much more conventional, starting in the 'real world' rather than a fantasy one, with an enigma set-up concerning a young man's missing father. The word 'father' is repeated throughout the trailer along with close-ups of the young hero's face to create an emotional attachment with the audience. One of the aims of the trailer is to minimise the sci-fi and fantasy element as this is likely to be off-putting to the mainstream audience viewing on these platforms.

In contrast to the use of synergy to target both niche and mainstream audiences, Fox's distribution of *Prometheus* shifted the emphasis from the multi-platform campaign associated with traditional synergy strategy to focus far more on online platforms. The stated aim of the campaign was to create an 'immersive' experience for the audience, rather than to rely on the traditional synergy strategy of trailer, poster and website. The trailers produced were primarily designed to be viewed through online platforms rather than TV. These were also non-conventional trailers which took the form of short films, such as 'David 8', a mock advertisement for the model of an android which features in the film. This 'trailer' deliberately blurs the boundary between a 'real' advert and the world of the film, perhaps making it difficult for an audience which does not understand that it is for a film to engage with.

'David 8' is filmed in a stylised way. There is restricted depth of field making it seem very flat, the colour is drained from the futuristic *mise en scène* and this flat effect is reinforced by the actor's performance as David, delivering the lines in a slightly creepy monotone voice. There is none of the enigma or narrative hints of a conventional trailer here; instead it links with the total *Prometheus* experience of code-breaking games and websites created for the fictional companies which appear in the film. The distribution of *Prometheus* suggests that synergy may be becoming less influential due to the power of convergence – distributers are no longer making distinctions between different media platforms associated with synergy but are instead aiming their marketing at an audience which is used to accessing all their media via smartphones or tablets.

Activity

Now take an example from your own case study and write a paragraph which analyses the different ways synergy has been used.

Remember the need to balance reference to institutions and products, to use media terminology and to address the question.

A SUCCESSFUL FILM CASE STUDY

The extract above only discusses two films and both of these are Hollywood blockbusters with similar budgets, both produced by global conglomerates. Despite the differences highlighted in style of marketing, this isn't enough to provide a wide range of examples as required by the assessment criteria. Therefore in the complete essay there would also need to be some reference to contrasting films, audiences and institutions. The following suggestions allow for a much greater contrast to be drawn with the blockbusters already discussed.

Winter's Bone

- US, low-budget, independent film
- Minimal marketing budget
- Limited online presence
- Emphasis on traditional release pattern: festivals, poster, website, word of mouth
- Critical acclaim
- Older, niche audience
- Impact of synergy: far more limited than for a blockbuster film; low budget for marketing means that print adverts and critical success are far more important for a successful campaign.

An overview of the distribution and marketing campaign for *Winter's Bone* 'Case Study: How Indie Hit "Winter's Bone" Came to Be' is available at: www.indiewire.com/article/toolkit_case_study_winters_bone.

Black Pond

- British, independent, micro budget film
- Distributed by the film makers rather than an institution
- Innovative exhibition strategy – film tour
- Minimal/no marketing budget
- Reliance on critical and festival acclaim
- Impact of synergy: even less than for *Winter's Bone* – publicity for *Black Pond* was initially reliant on hiring cinemas to show the film so that critics could review it. The subsequent positive reviews were the main element of the distribution campaign.

A detailed account of the financing, distribution and exhibition of *Black Pond* is at the official website, www.blackpondfilm.com/, which also links to a useful interview with one of the co-directors in Rushes Magazine: http://film.falmouth.ac.uk/2012/04/tom-kingsley-interview/.

By extending the range of the types of film in your cross-media study, it is clear that you can make many more points in relation to the essay question which should allow you to develop your argument in a more sophisticated way. By including an independent or micro-budget film it allows you to make the following points in considering the impact of synergy:

- A synergy strategy is more commonly used by blockbuster rather than independent films.
- Synergy is more appropriate to certain genres than others – character-driven dramas don't have many opportunities for synergy.

- Synergy is most effective when there is already awareness of the film.
- Not all platforms appeal equally to all audiences.
- The use of online platforms isn't free – websites cost to design, host and advertise.
- Synergy may have the effect of dominating the market so that small films are ignored.
- The impact of synergy may be in decline due to the emergence of convergence.

Writing exam essays

The ability to write a coherent, clearly-structured and argued essay is one of the ways in which your knowledge of the media is assessed in Section B of the exam. Essays follow their own codes and conventions which you need to learn in order to write a successful one. In this next section we will look at the 'rules' of essay writing and suggest some ways of learning to write successful essays – even in exam conditions.

1   *Exam essays must answer the question.* No doubt this is a very familiar instruction – you know that you must 'answer the question'. Despite this, students in exams routinely choose the wrong question to answer, begin by answering one question but veer towards addressing another as the essay develops or only make reference to the question in the introduction and conclusion.

   A common mistake is to put the question into 'your own words', although this may seem to help your understanding, it is dangerous as it is likely to move you away from the question focus. Remember the group of examiners who write the papers have spent a long time writing this essay question and every word has been carefully chosen. Therefore it is very important to understand the question before you start and to keep referring back to it throughout the writing of the essay.

2   Essays which summarise everything you know about an area without addressing the question explicitly will only gain a *low mark*. This is often the aspect of exam essay writing which is the most difficult to keep under control. It is also the case that it can seem a bit mean-spirited; if the question is about audiences and you describe the different target audiences from your case study then surely that demonstrates the work you've undertaken in the subject and should therefore gain credit? Unfortunately this always comes back to the first instruction – answer the question! This is the only way to show understanding (although of course the examiner will credit you for anything that you have included which is relevant).

Exam tip

Remind yourself of the exact wording of the question throughout the process of essay writing. It is easy in exam conditions to slightly change the question you are answering and this can result in you losing focus.

Typical mistakes of this kind are replacing one word from the question with another or to forget a specific instruction to 'evaluate' or 'assess' etc. For example, a recent question asked students to discuss *how* synergy was used in the cross-media study but then also to consider the *impact* of this use. As the essay developed many students forgot the focus on the second part, which prevented the answers from reaching the higher levels. Going back to the original wording will keep you focused on the question.

3   It is very important to spend time *planning your essay* in an exam – it's time well spent. A plan will help you to keep focused on the question, guide you in developing your argument and ensure that you don't forget an important point.

4   Before you start to plan your essay you need to make sure that you *choose the right question to answer*. In Section B there is only a choice of two, which may mean that you feel you could tackle either of them with some success – this actually makes the choice harder! In the report on the examination from June 2011, the principal examiner pointed out that many students chose to answer the question on institutions but actually wrote an essay on audiences, another reminder of the importance of reading the question carefully before you begin writing. In choosing the question it isn't always the case that the one that you like most or which seems easiest is the one you should answer. Remember (again!) that essays are a form of argument, so you should choose the question which allows you to develop the clearest argument using the most appropriate examples.

Exam tip

Which question? If you get a familiar question – perhaps you did a similar one in a mock or during revision – don't automatically choose it. There is a danger that your essay could become a rehash of the original one which will mean it's a bit dull and you may end up answering the previous question rather than the one in the exam.

Writing essays in an exam can be broken down into the following stages:

- read and analyse the essay title
- plan your answer
- write up your answer.

Read and analyse the essay title

It is important to read and analyse essay titles carefully. Initially you should see if the title can be broken down into a number of parts or questions. Underlining the key words and phrases is an ideal way to start. This will help you identify *what* you are being asked to discuss and *how* you are being asked to discuss it.

You know you will be asked to discuss media concepts and issues through reference to your specific cross-media study. However, you must note any specific directions which are included such as being asked to analyse, compare or evaluate; following these directions is what helps you gain the higher marks.

DIRECTIVE WORDS

There are a variety of directive words which can come up in an exam essay. Here are some of the most common along with a brief explanation of what they mean and how they are used.

Analyse   To separate or break up something into parts so that you can discuss it in detail. This will then mean that you can explain why it functions in the way it does – for example, by analysing your cross-media case study in detail you can explain how certain aspects of the media function.

Compare   Find similarities and differences between two or more media products, issues, critical approaches, etc. It is important to check whether you are being told what to compare or whether it is up to you to decide what would be the most relevant.

Contrast   There is a slight but important difference of emphasis between compare and contrast. Comparing something is about finding similarities and differences between things, but a 'contrast' directive term means that you should focus on the differences. Sometimes an essay question may ask you to both 'compare and contrast', in which case you know you have to do everything!

Discuss   If a question asks you to discuss something, you are being asked to present a point of view. This will include some description but the primary focus should be on interpretation. When discussing your cross-

essay terminology
You will feel much more confident in your essay writing if you are familiar with the structure of essay questions and how they are put together. Most essay questions will comprise the following:

- *key concepts and issues –* there will be a reference to the media concepts and current media issues and debates which tests your knowledge of the subject area.
- *directive or process words* this is an equally important aspect of the essay question as it tells you what you have to do in the essay. The directive word is what takes you beyond just describing your case study.

media study, you must ensure that your ideas are always supported by selected examples from your case study.

Evaluate   To evaluate is to present an opinion which is based on a consideration of different aspects of the area under focus. Similar to 'evaluate' are the phrases 'to what extent' or 'how true is . . .' – all these directional words ask you to consider opposing views so that you can assess the validity of the question or statement.

Exam tip

Because of the thousands of different cross-media studies undertaken by the students taking MEST1, the Section B essay questions will never refer to a specific media product, form or platform. Instead the question has to be written so that it can be answered whether you have studied film, sport, news, etc.

EXAMPLE: ANALYSING AN EXAM ESSAY QUESTION

To practice the stages of planning and writing an essay in an exam, read the following question from MEST1, June 2010:

'Audiences are becoming increasingly powerful in shaping media output.'

With reference to your case study, how far is this true?
    In your answer you should:

- provide a brief outline of your case study
- evaluate the roles of audiences in the creation of media products from your case study
- support your answer with reference to a range of examples from three media platforms.

This exam question follows a typical structure in that it puts forward a statement about the subject area and then asks you to consider to what extent the statement is true. The first stage of writing the essay is to analyse the key terms and instructions in the question. For this question your analysis should look something like this:

'<u>Audiences</u> are becoming increasingly <u>powerful</u> in <u>shaping media</u> output.'

With reference to your case study, **how far is this true**?

Support your answer with reference to a *range of examples* from *three media platforms*.

In this example three types of highlighting are used for the different types of terms used:

key media concepts and issues are underlined, the directive essay term is in bold, and the essay instructions are in italics.

Exam tip

If you get a 'quote' question like this, remember that you're not expected to recognise the quotation – it has been made up specifically for the exam, which is why there is no citation for it. The reason for structuring a question in this way is because it can provide a concise, provocative position, giving you something to argue against.

Activity

Looking at past paper questions is a very useful approach to revision – it helps to familiarise you with the style of questions as well as the different concepts which can be covered.

To get the most benefit from looking at past questions, put each question in the context of your topic area and ask yourself how it fits with the key issues and contemporary debates in Media Studies. The specific question in the exam will focus on one aspect of these areas (although it is likely to overlap with others too); when you understand the context, it makes your understanding of the question clearer.

Look at this question again and make a note of the media contexts it is referring to:

'Audiences are becoming increasingly powerful in shaping media output.'

Some suggestions:

- Increase in user-generated content enabled by new technology.
- Greater access to media without gatekeepers – for example, YouTube, blogs.

- Debates around role of amateur versus professional journalism.
- Simultaneous increase in domination of the media by global conglomerates.

Try this method with a range of other past paper questions which deal with different contexts. You will soon realise that by identifying the contexts you are also constructing a list of contemporary media issues.

It is worth taking a few minutes in the exam to bullet-point the context of the question – this should help you to develop your argument.

Plan your answer

People are often resistant to making plans for essays – particularly in exams when it might seem that there isn't enough time to both plan and write the essay. One trap students can fall into is thinking that because they didn't use a plan in the past and 'did okay' there is no need to start now. In response to this it is worth considering how much better the result might have been with some planning and also to acknowledge that at AS there is greater emphasis placed on the need to construct a logical argument than at GCSE.

However, it is also the case that you haven't got a long time to tackle Section B. Despite this, 5 minutes spent planning an essay will actually save you time. As a general rule you should spend around 10% of the allotted time on the plan. In the 45-minute time slot allocated to Section B, 4 or 5 minutes spent on planning would therefore be a reasonable amount of time.

Once you have carefully analysed the title, allow yourself some time to write down any and all ideas which you think are associated with it. This free-flow of ideas is sometimes described as a 'thought shower'. Don't worry about getting them in any order or making them completely clear. The idea is to simply gather your thoughts in one place.

WHICH TYPE OF PLAN WORKS FOR YOU?

Mind maps or spider diagrams. These are examples of visual plans which gather all your ideas onto one page, focusing on the key terms and issues around the question. The advantage of this type of planning is that it is quick and fluid – it's easy to add to it as you go along. Many students find this a helpful way to get ideas flowing when faced with a blank sheet of paper. On its own this type of plan doesn't provide the step-by-step structure of an introduction, main body and conclusion but you could provide this by numbering the different arms of the diagram in the order they should be used.

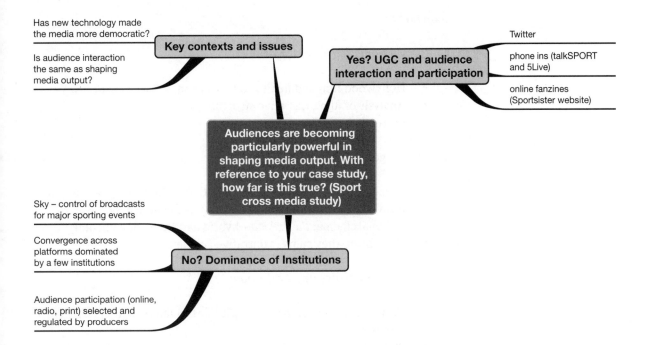

Has new technology made the media more democratic?

Is audience interaction the same as shaping media output?

Key contexts and issues

Yes? UGC and audience interaction and participation

Twitter

phone ins (talkSPORT and 5Live)

online fanzines (Sportsister website)

Audiences are becoming particularly powerful in shaping media output. With reference to your case study, how far is this true? (Sport cross media study)

Sky – control of broadcasts for major sporting events

Convergence across platforms dominated by a few institutions

No? Dominance of Institutions

Audience participation (online, radio, print) selected and regulated by producers

Figure 8
Essay plan mind map.

Alternatively this could be used as a first stage before moving to a linear plan.

Linear notes and bullet points. This type of plan lists headings and key points. It would usually be organised around the three main stages of an essay – the introduction, main body and conclusion – with each section having numbered subheadings which refer to the number of paragraphs in each section. The number of paragraphs will obviously vary but a guide would be one paragraph each for the introduction and conclusion with three to five in the main body.

The key to a successful linear plan is that you keep it brief – don't end up with complete sentences for each point as you will end up writing the essay twice.

EXAMPLE OF A LINEAR PLAN

'All media texts tell stories'. In what ways is narrative used in the media products in your case study?

(Film case study)
Introduction

• Define narrative in relation to the different media forms in case study
• Address 'what ways' – what are some of the aims of narrative?

Main body

1   Conventional narrative forms:

  - Hollywood film and institution – romcom – *Friends with Benefits*
  - Analysis of film's narrative structure
  - Poster as narrative form.

2   Challenges to conventional narrative:

  - Puzzle films: *Inception* and *Source Code* – link to narrative games (scavenger hunt) and the introduction of characters on website
  - National cinema: *Black Pond* – hybrid narratives, documentary forms
  - How far do they subvert narrative conventions?

3   Narrative, audience and institution:

  - Narrative structure as ideological/associated with specific institutions
  - Pleasures for the audience in reassurance of narrative structure and in subversion – refer to audience blogs, review references to narrative.

Conclusion

  - Summarise the different ways media products from your case study tell stories (structures)
  - Summarise the reasons for and effects of these narratives.

The plan you complete at the beginning of the essay will probably not be perfect and may change as you start to write the essay itself. However, having a plan to hand makes it much easier to see how you need to alter the structure or include further points etc. than if you were writing without one.

Creating an effective structure

As you know, an essay consists of three parts, an introduction, main body and conclusion, and each section has its own function.

THE INTRODUCTION

Although approaches to this part of the essay can vary, here is an approach which is particularly effective in putting the person reading your essay (in this case the examiner) at ease. First, show clearly that you're responding to the essay title. State what you are going to do in the essay in a few short, clear sentences. This will help to give your essay a clear structure for the reader to follow. Finally, tell the reader what you are going to argue or conclude.

Exam tip

When you're writing an essay for an exam, or as part of your coursework, the introduction is incredibly important in setting out your argument. The introduction outlines what you are going to argue or conclude. Make this clear from the start rather than keeping the reader in suspense. Once your argument is clear then the main body provides the evidence for this position.

The following points provide some suggestions for writing a successful introduction. Practising these approaches will mean that it will become much easier to use these techniques in the exam – it will be second nature.

1   Get the reader's interest

The examiner will of course pay great attention to your work, but think how much keener they will be to read your essay if it starts with a thoughtful, original and relevant point rather than merely repeating the essay question. A successful opening sentence demonstrates your knowledge and understanding – and also your confidence and interest in the subject.

> *Avoid:* In this essay I will discuss the idea that audiences are becoming increasingly powerful in shaping media output.

What do you think is wrong with starting an essay like this? Imagine you're the examiner. What does this sentence tell you about the student's knowledge and understanding? The answer would have to be 'nothing really' because it is merely repeating the question. You won't lose any marks by opening your essay in this way, but neither will you gain any – and you have perhaps planted a seed of doubt in the examiner's mind as to whether you actually know anything about this topic area.

Instead you could try something like this:

Fifteen million telephone votes were cast by audience members during the seventh season of *X Factor*, resulting in the singer Matt Cardle winning the ITV talent show competition.

As an opening sentence this is far more interesting and lively but it also immediately demonstrates to the examiner that you are thinking about the question. The sentence sets up an example of ways that audiences shape media output (being responsible for the winner of *X Factor*) but it also introduces a challenge to the idea of audience power which you can refer back to – is Matt Cardle a successful star?

2   *Introduce the topic*

The next part of the introduction – probably two or three sentences at most – should explain your first statement, and prepare the examiner for the rest of the essay, in particular your argument.

The phenomenon of audience participation – in this case through voting – across a variety of reality and lifestyle programmes is one of the reasons for the current debate in media studies about the role of the audience. This debate is concerned with whether the audience has, through new technology and increased media expertise, become more powerful or whether the dominance of global media institutions means that the idea of the more active audience is an illusion.

3   *Address the question and make your argument clear*

The final line of the introduction should 'answer' the question and lead the reader into the next paragraph – hopefully because they want to find out what you're going to say next:

In studying a range of examples of reality TV programming it is clear that while audiences are more visible in the media than ever before, they actually have minimal influence in shaping the output of TV institutions.

A successful introduction demonstrates your knowledge and engagement. The fact that it directly refers to the question shows that you're thinking about the topic, not just regurgitating something you've learnt by rote.

THE MAIN BODY OF THE ESSAY

This is the major part of your essay, as your introduction and conclusion should only be one paragraph each. Typically, you might have three or four points of discussion in the main body, although this can vary depending on the essay. For each point explain clearly the subject under discussion. Remember to keep showing how your points are directly addressing the essay title and how it is related to the argument you made in the introduction.

In each paragraph try to follow the 'main point, plus supporting evidence and conclusion' structure. That is, state the main point that you are making at the start of the paragraph, then give your evidence and/or reasoning in support of this point and then refer back to the main point again as you conclude your paragraph.

1   Example of a main idea

Developments in technology have created more possibilities for audience involvement in media production.

2   Offer evidence to support this statement

It is now possible to film, edit and distribute a film on a smartphone; sites such as YouTube provide a platform to exhibit media products without having to wait to be bought by a studio. Recent fan films such as the non-profit independent production *The Hunt for Gollum*, a prequel to the Lord of the Rings trilogy, have been both popular and critical successes.

3   You should then include further examples and evidence . . .

This shift, where audiences become performers and producers, is also apparent on television. In 2012 Channel 4 commissioned a comedy sketch show called *The Midnight Beast*. The show developed out of a YouTube site which had received 40 million hits and includes parodies of music videos and other aspects of youth culture.

4   . . . before linking to the next paragraph

Both these examples demonstrate the increasing power of the audience in shaping media products, but it could also be argued that these are very specific type of media – aimed at a young, male, fan-boy audience.

The next paragraph would then look at whether or not this is a phenomenon that is wider than this one audience.

THE CONCLUSION

This should be brief and to the point, and no more than a paragraph in length. You should aim to summarise your essay by gathering the most important of the points that you have made. This summary can then be used to justify your main argument or conclusion, as stated in the introduction:

> Developments in digital technologies and the advent of synergy and convergence have had great implications for the role of the audience and their relationship to media producers and institutions. These developments have been particularly marked in the areas of reality TV and those forms which appeal to a young, niche audience. In all these examples, however, it is arguable whether audiences really have any meaningful power in shaping media output. This is due to the increasing dominance of media conglomerates which still exert a great degree of control over what is produced and how it is consumed.

Exam tip

It's impossible to say how many pages you should write for your answer. As a guide the exam paper has five sheets for a Section B response. The only real answer to this question is that you should write as much as you can in the time but that it all needs to be relevant.

It is very hard to get into the top levels if you've only written two sides but writing ten pages probably means that you have lost focus and are just writing down everything you know about the case study – and anything else which comes to mind! Once again a clear plan will help you to write the right amount.

If you know you tend to write too much, cut down the number of individual points in your plan. If you find it difficult to write enough, expand on some of your points with subpoints in the planning stage.

Revision tip

You don't have to write complete essay-length answers to every question when you're revising. It's also useful to write parts of a question. For example:

- write introductions and conclusions
- do a plan for the whole answer
- place the question in context and list key points to mention
- discuss and compare approaches to specific questions with other students
- practise writing the first sentence of the paragraphs for the main body
- swap essays with fellow students, use the mark scheme (available on the exam board website) to mark them and explain why you have put the essay into a specific level.

Activity

All the emphasis in your revision so far has been on you as a student facing an unseen exam, but at this advanced stage of your revision it is useful to take a different perspective – that of the person who writes the exam questions. To write an exam question you need to have in-depth knowledge of the specification, knowledge of a range of contemporary media products and an excellent understanding of contemporary media – just as you should at this stage in your preparation.

Writing an exam question is useful because it helps you to focus on exactly what you are expected to know and what you're supposed to do with this knowledge.

How to write an exam question

1   What are you testing? Go back and look at the Assessment Outcomes for the topic or section. In this case they are the ability to apply knowledge and understanding when analysing media products and processes to show how meanings and responses are created. The questions are designed to assess candidates' ability to apply their knowledge and understanding of the products and processes in their chosen topic area across the range of media platforms, and to explore how meanings and responses are created.

In other words, by the time you've finished your AS course and are preparing to sit the exam you should be able to do all of these things. The trick is to write a question which allows the student to demonstrate that they can do them all.

2   Writing good essay questions

- Formulate the question so that the task is clearly defined for the student. Make sure that the directive words are clear; sometimes the use of 'Discuss' or 'Explain' are a bit vague. Remember you want the student (you!) to be able to do as well as possible and therefore not be confused by the wording.
- Avoid questions that only require factual knowledge such as 'Describe the organisation of a public service broadcaster in your cross-media study'.
- Essays are used to test 'higher level' skills such as application and analysis (rather than just memory), so therefore directional terms such as 'compare' or 'evaluate' are likely to be more appropriate than 'define' or 'describe'.
- Make your questions as concise as possible and identify one main idea which you want to focus on – choosing one of the media concepts to test will help here.

The final step: taking the exam

If you've worked your way through the two revision sections on MEST1, you now – hopefully – feel fully ready and confident. At this point you probably just want to get the exam over with. As you are probably well aware there is no quick and easy solution to doing well in exams. The best guarantee is to be as prepared as possible and this of course means having to do all the hard work which gets you to this stage. You may want to go back to the introduction and read through the section 'Making examiners happy' for a reminder of best exam practice but otherwise try to relax, get a good night's sleep and remember – the exam is designed for you to demonstrate what you know, not to try to trip you up. Good luck!

PART 3

A2 LEVEL

INTRODUCING A2

The challenge of A2

So you have managed to get this far – well done! The good news is that you have probably done the hard bit in getting through the AS component of the course. The A2 bit should be comparatively plain sailing.

> ## Tip
>
> GCE exams were once all assessed at the end of two years of the course. The qualification was then spilt into AS and A2 in order to give students a goal to aim at for the end of the first year. It follows that your A2 exam is going to be more demanding and more complex (in other words harder) than your AS exam. Understanding the ways in which A2 is harder will help you significantly in your preparation for it.

So what is A2 all about? Well, in essence it develops the skills that you learned at AS so that you are able to apply them with a greater degree of sophistication than you were in the first year of your course. Of course, you may well think that you didn't really develop any skills doing AS other than your ability to pass exams. This is a good point, therefore, at which to look back over the work you did for AS and make an audit of the skills that you developed. These can be summarised as follows:

- A grasp of the key concepts that informed a great deal of your AS work.
- The ability to analyse products using these key concepts.
- Production skills in creating your media product for MEST.
- Evaluative skills in terms of both your own productions and mass media output.

> **NOTE**
>
> With any luck you will have remembered the key concepts. Just in case you have had such a good summer that you have forgotten, here is a brief summary of them.
>
> - Representations
> - Institutions
> - Media Language, Genre and Narrative
> - Audience
> - Values and Ideology.

In addition to the Media Studies skills that you developed above, your first year of study should also have taught you a lot of other skills that are going to come in particularly handy for tackling A2. These skills include:

- *Study skills*. You will have learned how to study and the particular approaches that are most effective in studying the media. There is a section reminding you of these on p. 129.
- *Research skills*. These are going to become especially important at A2 level as you develop more and more independence in your learning.
- *Essay writing skills*. Remember the skill you developed for writing essays under exam conditions. You are going to need those again.
- *Your ability to work autonomously*. Remember, that means your ability (and willingness) to go off on your own and explore both media products and the issues that they raise.

This is a good point at which to subject yourself to a 'SWOT' analysis. SWOT stands for:

- Strengths
- Weaknesses
- Opportunities
- Threats.

A SWOT analysis is about standing back for a moment and making an honest assessment of what you have achieved and what you need to do to achieve even more. Using the two lists above, try to identify under these headings exactly what strengths and weaknesses you have exhibited and what opportunities and threats might result from these. Put more simply, identify the things you think you are good at and those that you think you are not so good at.

Of course it is no good just leaving it at that. The things you are good at present opportunities. For example, if you think you are good at research skills, A2 will provide you with lots of opportunities for developing these skills beyond the immediate confines of Media Studies as well as into wider contexts which we will look at in a moment. More importantly, you need to confront any perceived weaknesses in your skills base. It is no good being brilliant at research if you can't write essays; the two go hand in hand. If you can't write essays, then find someone who can help you. At the very least you should take time to read the sections covering exam technique in this book and its companion: *A2 Media Studies: The Essential Introduction for AQA* (second edition) by Antony Bateman, Peter Bennett, Sarah Casey-Benyahia, Jacqui Shirley and Peter Wall (2010), London: Routledge.

So how is A2 different from AS?

The whole AQA GCE Media Studies qualification relies heavily on ideas centred around the analysis of media products. The units at A2 are no exception. Analysis and the application of the key concepts to this analysis remain absolutely central to your success or failure. You do, however, need to be aware of some new dimensions that have an impact on the way in which A2 units are assessed. These are:

- wider contexts
- theoretical perspectives
- synopticity.

You will read a good deal more about these as we look closely at the demands of MEST3. It is useful though to take a brief look at them here so you can get thinking about how you are going to deal with them.

Wider contexts

Media products do not exist in a vacuum, even though exam boards like to encapsulate them into exam papers and make you analyse them. Media products are both created and consumed as part of a complex social and cultural organisation in which we live. Media products both reflect and influence the society and culture they exist in. This is one reason why Media Studies is not only interesting but also important. The nature of media products, the output of media institutions and the consumption of media audiences all provide important barometers of the concerns, values and neuroses of the culture in which we live. Studying the media is, therefore, one way of gaining valuable insight into the very nature of culture.

So, wider contexts as they relate to A2 are the cultural and social conditions that exist at a time a media product is produced and consumed.

NOTE

Why is there so much reality television on our screens? Possible answers:

- That's what people want to watch.
- Producers find it cheap to make and have the production facilities, such as the Big Brother house, set up and ready to use.
- Society is sick and voyeuristic and enjoys seeing the pain and suffering of others.

- In the digital age there are just too many hours of air time to fill, so broadcasters like any programme that is cheap and fills up huge amounts of this air time.
- Bad television is just so ironic.

Notice that none of the above answers is directly related to reality television programmes. Each offers a wider context, either in terms of production, audience consumption or the nature of our culture and society. So when you are asked to explore 'wider contexts' as part of your A2 course, this is the sort of area you need to be looking at: the contexts of production and consumption as well as the broader cultural and social contexts that influence the nature of a media product and in turn are likely to be influenced by it.

Hang on to the stuff about irony – you may want to think about that later.

NOTE

One of the aims of the specification is for students to:

develop and formulate their approach to the media and the role of the media in today's society by referring in detail to the wider contexts (social, political, historical, economic, as appropriate) which affect media production, distribution and exhibition.

You may have noticed a problem. In a nutshell – how are you supposed to get at these wider contexts? You may have noticed an even bigger problem. How are you supposed to write about these wider contexts in an exam when it will be the first time you have seen these products?

Of course there is no simple answer to either question. The first is probably the easier of the two. You need to do some research. That means you need to do some digging around to get to the background information that you need about products and issues you are exploring.

Fortunately there is something built into the specification to help you. It is called MEST4: Critical Investigation. By the time you read this you will probably know a fair bit about it. You will know that you are expected to take a product, theme or debate which is relevant to the contemporary media landscape and produce a 2,000-word study of it. Following the guidance in the specification, you will appreciate that this is a product-based study, that is, it has to be rooted in some element of media output as its starting point. What you are then expected to do is to work outwards from the product in order to access wider contexts of the type we explored above.

With any luck you will be reading this before you embark on your Critical Investigation. If you have already completed MEST4, all is not lost however. Your choice of topic for the Critical Investigation unit can have a key bearing on what you need to do to prepare for your MEST3. It can help specifically by enabling you to do some background research into at least one of the topics you are preparing for in MEST3. This is where you need to enter into a discussion with the teacher who is supervising your Critical Investigation and the teacher who is preparing you for the MEST3 exam, if these are not the same person.

An obvious example might be focusing on some aspect of news gathering and presentation of news or your MEST4 topic so that you have ready-prepared material for use in the MEST3 exam. Similarly most media output you look at is likely to raise issues of new media and identity, so you should see here a potential overlap with one or both of these MEST3 topic areas.

Theoretical perspectives

perspectives
This term is used to describe ways of looking at things. Perspective is a means of adding depth and complexity to your analysis of media output by providing you with a vantage point or lens for looking at and exploring it. So to see a media product from a feminist perspective is a way of seeing how that product can be interpreted in relation to the empowerment or disempowerment of women in a culture generally dominated by men.

Your study of the media should have made you aware of the vast extent to which it is used socially. Media output is a common talking point whenever people meet and exchange ideas. Just about everyone has something to say about the media, especially contemporary topics such as the latest reality TV show or a controversial new film showing at the cinema. On this basis, the majority of the population could wander into a Media Studies exam room and have a go at many of the questions on the paper. Some of the better informed might even scrape a pass. The reason that they would probably fail, however, is that their knowledge and understanding of the media would lack the important theoretical framework that is central to an academic study of the media. It is this theoretical base that you need to be able to demonstrate that is an important ingredient of your success at A2.

Of course at this point you are hoping for a list of key theories that you can learn and show off in the exam. You have probably guessed, however, that being Media Studies it is not quite that simple. There is a list coming up you will be glad to hear, but it is not the sort of thing that you can just learn and trot out in the exam. Let's try to explain why.

The history of cultural studies, the larger discipline of which Media Studies is a part, is littered with theories, many of which are now quite outmoded not least because of changes in the way technology has influenced the production and consumption of media products. Roughly we can identify a continuum running from the early propaganda models of the Frankfurt

School through to postmodern notions of media and personal identity. Most theories by their nature are designed to explore products and issues from a specific point of view. Far from being an objective take, they seek to put forward and support a particular perspective from which to consider media output. A good example of this would be feminist theory.

Feminist theory sees the media and its products from the perspective of women. Clearly this is a complex issue, but at a simple level many media products can be interpreted through their ideological function of supporting and preserving the patriarchal social order in which power is vested in men. Media products can be seen as a mechanism for controlling women in order to ensure they remain in a position in society which is subordinate to men. A survey of advertising, for example, by a feminist would point to the representation of women in advertisements in a comparatively limited number of roles compared to those represented by men. The conclusion might be that the media do this in order to gain our acceptance that this is natural or inevitable and therefore in some way acceptable or 'right'.

Here is a list of some of the theories that you could well find useful in exploring A2 topics. It is not exhaustive but there again it's not prescriptive either. There are other useful theories and some useful theories are not necessarily included. It is meant to be a way of guiding you into the intelligent use of theory for A2. If you want to do a proper job of learning about theory, then read the chapter 'Theoretical Perspectives' in *A2 Media Studies: The Essential Introduction*. It will provide you with a greater appreciation of the complexity of these important perspectives.

You will perhaps recognise that we are back at the point we argued earlier in this section about everyone having some kind of opinion on the media. It is your grasp of and ability to apply theory that will separate your arguments and insights from the informed non-specialist. So you had better learn some if you have not done so already.

So here is our top ten of media/cultural theories for you to brush up on:

1 *Semiotics*. If you don't know that semiotics is the study of signs by now, then sell this book and get a job.
2 *Post-structuralism*. Some interesting stuff here. This perspective takes semiotics and says that looking for meaning is pretty pointless because it is just about impossible to pin down meaning anyway. This position privileges hugely the consumers of media products, audiences, as it is they who ultimately give a media product such meaning as it has.
3 *Postmodernism*. An especially useful perspective which develops ideas from post-structuralism to argue that the divide between high and popular culture is irrelevant or even non-existent and there are no real unifying theories anyway because culture and society have become so fragmented.

4 *Feminism*. As a perspective for looking at media products, feminists would see most media output as being the product of a patriarchal or male-dominated order aimed at disempowering women.

5 *Queer theory*. As its name suggests, queer theory is concerned with sexuality and identity. It sees gender as being constructed socially and to some degree through our association with the media. It would be useful to consider some of the ways in which gender identity is represented in mainstream mass media output.

6 *Marxism*. It does seem a bit unfair to the world's greatest political thinker to reduce his views to a single bullet point. In media terms, Marxism is probably best seen through class war. A Marxist view of the media would be that mass media output functions as a means of keeping the proletariat, or working class, in its place to preserve the power of the capitalist ruling elite; much media output is simply a diversion to deflect the workers from rising up against the power elite. You might like to check this idea out by reading a copy of the *Sun*.

7 *Liberal pluralism*. This perspective sees the mass media as being generally positive in its influence on society. It makes a play of individual choice and freedom which a free media does a lot to maintain in a democratic society. Liberal pluralism provides a handy place for liberal left-wing intellectuals to sit on the fence.

8 *Post-colonialism*. With many of the global issues raised by the Bush/Blair invasion of Iraq, post-colonialism becomes an increasingly important perspective. Basically it identifies the role of the media in the Western domination of developing countries not least through the export of Western culture and social, economic and political systems to them.

9 *Audience theory*. There is a range of audience theory which looks at the relationship between audience and the media. At one extreme is the Frankfurt School, which argues that the audience are passive and vulnerable, whereas more recent theory is interested in how the audience uses the media, and is active, or even interactive.

10 *Genre theory*. Genre is a useful tool for exploring the relationship between the structure of a media product, the producer and the audience. This perspective seeks to identify the formulae which inform the production of media products, and how they can evolve to reflect the wider social, cultural and industrial context.

Activity

A good activity you might undertake is to choose a product that you know reasonably well and to work through the list of perspectives to see how each might offer some insight into that product. Try to make a habit of this each time you look at a product, perhaps just choosing two or three perspectives that seem particularly appropriate and looking at how they might be applied.

So, here's a brief recap on getting down to A2 study:

- Don't forget that the specification is still very product-centred. That means that you should always make products your starting point and a constant reference point when exploring ideas, issues and debates.
- You need to get a handle on wider contexts. These are the contexts of production and consumption as well as the wider social, political, historical and economic contexts that shape the nature of media products.
- You need to learn to apply theory. If you are going to do really well, you need to apply it both appropriately and with confidence.
- You need to identify and discuss relevant media issues and debates, applying them across the media.

Finally, there is a section in Part 4 at the end of this book explaining to you how the exams that you take are set and marked. It is at the back of the book because if you don't have to read it, we didn't want it to get in the way. If you have time, however, give it a quick once- over. There is some useful information in there that should help give you an insight into the exam process. It should also help you prepare for your exams by detailing some of the ground rules that examiners follow when they set exams. As you will see there are strict limits on what can and cannot be set. These are determined by what is laid down in the specification which you can access on the AQA website. If you are prepared to do a bit of research into this, you should go into the exam room just a bit better prepared for what is waiting for you.

Synopticity

This rather cumbersome word refers to a feature which is found in a wide range of A level specifications, typically in the final module, covering a breadth of subject areas. The synoptic element of media can be broken down into three parts.

Synopticity
In assessment terms this means the drawing together of the different strands of the qualification you are taking. As you would guess, synopticity is important in the final stages of your course.

1   Reference to and fluent use of the key concepts of the subject as tools of analysis.
2   Drawing together the learning you have completed throughout the specification, and using it as appropriate. Time, therefore, to brush up on some of your AS learning perhaps!
3   Placing media products and the associated issues and debates into their contexts and recognising they are affected by the contexts. Examples of these wider contexts are historical contexts (very noticeable in, for example 1970s situation comedy, which is full of material which reflects the sensitivities of the time period and which we may find odd or in many cases offensive in our modern eyes) or cultural contexts (as seen in any film or TV programme made in a country culturally dissimilar to the UK, where again, our Westernised experiences may be at odds with the experiences shown in the product).

What kind of student have you become?

In Part 2, you may remember that we asked the question: What kind of student are you? We divided students into two categories – active and passive. We explained that passive students were a real pain to teach because they were so heavily reliant on their teacher. They expected their teacher to do everything for them, including thinking. Ideally they would quite like their teacher to take the exam for them, providing of course that they managed to get a decent grade. We suggested that passive students were unlikely to do as well as they might expect at AS level because Media Studies is a discipline which seeks to reward students who do not rely on their teacher too heavily. It rewards students who are prepared to think for themselves.

You may remember that these students who think for themselves are called active students. You could have got the impression that we like active students. Well, you would be right. Active students are a pleasure to teach because they *want* to learn. They have enquiring minds that enjoy finding out about things. In Media Studies this should translate into a desire to seek out media products and to try applying some of the ideas that have been explored in class to them. Always bear in mind that you are very lucky to be able to study the media. Media products are nearly always accessible and nearly always enjoyable. These are the raw materials of your programme of study. This is certainly not bad when you can spend an evening watching *Dr Who* or going to the cinema and you can call it homework, provided of course you think about what you have seen, analyse how meaning has been created through a combination of visual and technical codes and apply the appropriate theory to it.

With any luck if you started without the level of autonomy that you need to be an active student, you will have developed this to some degree by the time you are studying at A2. If you have not, then here is a serious suggestion: do something else. Without the ability to learn independently, you are wasting your time doing A2 Media Studies. The whole of the A2 assessment is geared towards your ability to do things for yourself. Relying wholly on your teacher is a great way to do badly.

So why is this the case? Well, as you will read in the next section, the transition from AS study to A2 study is marked by a shift from analysis focused on the product to an application of wider contexts and theoretical perspectives. Put simply, you are shifting away from study of the product in its own right to looking at media products in a broader way. You will have to look at the context in which media products are produced and consumed. You will also have to look at some of the theoretical issues that underpin our study of the media at this level. This is a tall order and poses a challenge for which you need to be prepared.

So how do you start to tackle it? Well, the key is developing your skills in independent research. Now fortunately this is one place where the A2 specification rallies round to help you. Ironically the key to your success in A2 exams lies in the coursework unit MEST4, also known as Critical Perspectives. MEST4 requires you to produce a 2,000-word essay on a topic of your choice. The basic limitations are that your study is product based and contemporary. This means that you have to take as your starting point contemporary media output and use it to explore some wider issues in terms of contemporary media.

Activity

There is nothing to stop you choosing a topic for MEST4 that will overlap with at least one of your areas of study for MEST3. Given that MEST4 is made up of some pretty wide possibilities, finding overlaps should not be too strenuous. Topics such as new/digital media and audience and identity are obviously central to most media products, so it makes sense to see how you may use your MEST4 study topic as the basis for further exploration in MEST3.

Your choice of case study is an important consideration. The studies you will undertake will form a large part of your preparation for the MEST3 examination and so the first thing to perhaps consider is to choose something you have an interest in and, as we have just mentioned, this may help to inform your choices for the practical work you complete for MEST4.

The sections later in this book on the case studies for MEST3 will offer further advice on choosing your topic but remember that no matter how interested in a topic you are, or how passionate you are about it or how influential you see this aspect of the topics covered, you will need to research deeply into both primary and secondary sources and to consider the topic from numerous angles and perspectives. This might mean that your passion for the topic which you possess prior to commencing your case study is tested, as it consumes your media classwork and homework.

Further to this, your case studies are product-based, which is to say you will need to consume and consider a wide range of media products covering a variety of media platforms. Your research into these products needs to be conducted in context and throughout this revision guide we will consider how you might go about the sometimes difficult task of seeking out contexts. For the moment, however, just get your head around the thought that if you want to do well at A2, you will need to be both independent in your choice of media products to explore and show the ability to explore the contexts that relate to these products. The contexts are primarily production ones but can also relate to the consumption of media output.

Activity

Imagine you are looking at the following possible topics to explore for MEST3. Identify some of the key media products that you think it would be useful to consider. Then identify some of the contexts that you think might be important to understanding further the nature of these products:

- Reality television
- Celebrity news stories
- Digital technology and audiences
- Gossip magazines
- Films based on computer games
- The music industry

The other big issue at A2 is theory. Media Studies is a discipline full of theories. On one level this is great news because it allows you lots of opportunities for looking at theoretical perspectives. Any product you look at is likely to lend itself to a range of different tools with which to prise it open. Marxist, feminist or postmodernist theories are all likely to be applicable to the products that you want to explore.

Of course, theories exist for no other purpose than to be shot down. Or at least it might seem so to you. Perhaps you are not quite at the stage of your academic career when you feel equipped to challenge the major theorists, but what you are in a position to do is to question the validity of the theories that you come across. More simply, you are in a position to question whether they are theories that are true on the basis of the products that you have studied.

Don't forget you are studying Media Studies at a time when the discipline is in a state of flux. A lot of the theories and ideas that have been taken for granted for many years are being questioned, not least because they have become outdated in the face of the vast technological changes that have taken place in the way in which media products are both produced and consumed. The case study options for MEST3 are in some ways chosen to reflect this as in new/digital media and identity they represent some of the most rapidly changing areas of the discipline.

In his introduction to Web studies (*Web Studies: Rewiring Media Studies for the Digital Age* by David Gauntlett (ed.) (2000), London: Hodder and Stoughton), David Gauntlett describes Media Studies research at the end of the twentieth century as having entered 'a middle-aged, stodgy period'. He says it wasn't 'really sure what it could say about things any more'. He goes on to list some of the reasons why Media Studies has encountered these problems. You may well find it useful to check out what they are in *Media Studies: The Essential Resource* by Philip Rayner, Peter Wall and Stephen Kruger (eds) (2004), London: Routledge.

NOTE

One thing that you should find in your research is that there are many opportunities to question the theories that form the basis for the Media Studies textbooks that you have been using. The hallmark of a really good active Media Studies student at A2 is this willingness to question what has gone before. That does not mean that you have a licence to go round rubbishing every theory you have encountered. There will be theoretical issues that you will feel remain useful and have an important application today. Equally you must realise that it is not an act of heresy to call into question some of the received wisdom that underpins Media Studies. You need to adopt a healthy scepticism about the ideas that you come across. Better still be prepared to test them out against your own experience of media output and its contexts.

With any luck, then, you will have decided at AS to be an active student. At A2 you will now have to develop and extend your abilities as an active student. If you don't, here is a dire warning of what might happen.

Section A of the MEST3 exam is about thinking on your feet. It is a really stiff and demanding test of how good you are at applying what you have learned. If you go into the exam stuck at the same level of analysis as you were at AS, you will do badly. In Section A of the exam, examiners are looking for a sophisticated response; the type of response that comes from being able to engage with the products, contexts and theories in the way that only an active student can.

In Section B of the MEST3 exam your examiner will probably find very little evidence of learning because you will rely too heavily on the materials the teachers have taught you. Your answers will appear as though they have been learned by rote and they will be very similar to if not the same as everyone else's in the class taking the exam. You will also find it difficult to respond to the actual question you are trying to answer in the exam. This is because you will not be flexible enough to adapt what you know to the question you are asked. Typically a passive student ignores the question and writes down what they have been told in class. That is a bad idea.

The MEST4 Critical Investigation is your real chance to pursue an aspect of Media Studies that really interests you. There is very little limitation on what you can explore as long as it is focused on media output and is contemporary. You would have to be mad to ignore the opportunities it presents.

Active or passive – the choice is yours

Finally, you have probably been nursed through A level by a caring teacher prepared to spend time with you when you needed extra help. The next stop is university, where staff are very unlikely to spend extra time with you. It is sink or swim once you get there. Active students make pretty good swimmers.

Revising for A2 exams

If you have got this far in your exam-taking career, you must know something about revising for exams. There again, you may have just been lucky – these things happen. Assuming that your success to date is attributable to your own efforts in terms of study and revision rather than luck, this is a good point at which to review what you are doing right and what you may be able to do better.

Look back over the AS level exam. You will remember that it consisted of Section A, analysis of an 'unseen' media product, and Section B, the cross-media study. You had to revise for both of these sections but it is likely that you felt it necessary to spend more time focused on revision for Section B than for Section A. The reason for this is that Section B requires you to bring rather more information to the exam than Section A.

Revision for AS exams consisted, therefore, of a combination of:

- learning and knowing how to apply concepts, specifically the key concepts
- finding examples of appropriate case studies to exemplify your conceptual and contextual understanding.

You looked at concepts and media output in parallel with one another so that in Section A you felt confident in applying the concepts to an unseen product and in Section B you were able to talk about the concepts, theories, issues and debates, and show your understanding of them through the use of case studies that you had studied in preparation for the exam.

The good news is that the same basic principles should underpin your revision for the A2 exams. Indeed you will find that the exams that you take at A2 are disconcertingly similar to those you took at AS. Don't be fooled, however, into thinking that your revision strategy should be exactly the same. As you will have read in the introduction, although A2 may look the same, it makes significantly different demands on you. If you are smart, these different demands will become the prime focus of your revision.

Before we look at how to tackle these different demands, let's just remind you of some of the broad principles of revision in case you missed them first time round.

Organising your notes

The number one job when revising is to get your notes sorted out. By this point in your A level study you should be good at taking notes. If you aren't, then it is time you learned. Of course being good at taking notes and keeping them organised are two different things. Notes that are not organised need to be organised sharpish if they are to be any good. So the first thing you need to do is read through your notes to make sure that they make sense. If there are serious omissions, then deal with this. You can do this either by swapping notes with other people in your class or finding the right resources and making the notes you have missed.

One skill you should have developed by now is the ability to make notes on media products that have interested you and/or seem relevant to a particular area of study. Don't forget that some of the products that you have studied for AS will also be relevant here. You may need to revisit and extend them to meet the demands of A2, but that may be easier than starting from scratch.

You will also need to get down useful notes from other sources. These will include textbooks and websites. One thing you must learn to be aware of here is the dangers of plagiarism. Your teacher will have warned you about this in relation to the Critical Investigation you have prepared for MEST4. You will remember that if you quote from other sources, then you are obliged to acknowledge the source that you have used. Clearly in coursework copying is much more of an issue than in an exam. However, bear in mind that in an exam it is always a good idea to acknowledge ideas that you have used from sources other than your own head. One very good reason for doing this is to let the examiner know that you have engaged with some of theories surrounding the topic you are writing about. Don't forget, therefore, in your notes to write down details of the sources you have used so that you will at least be able to mention the name of the author in the exam. In addition it may be that as part of your revision you may wish to go back to the original source to expand your notes.

> **NOTE**
>
> One skill you should have developed in your work on the Independent Study is the use of Harvard referencing. You can read up on the detail on p. 34 of *A2 Media Studies* if you do not know already. While it is both unnecessary and inappropriate to use the Harvard system in an exam, there is a lot to be said for adopting this notation for citing sources in your notes. It will certainly help you when you get to higher education and find yourself writing this sort of extended essay on a regular basis.

If you are going to do well at A2 level, good notes are absolutely essential. One reason for this is that you are going to collect a lot of background information that you may need to help you in your exam answers. This is especially the case in Section B of the exam where a lot of preparation has to be made in advance if you are going to produce decent answers to the questions you tackle. The sort of background that is particularly important is contextual information about the products that you are studying. In the section on wider contexts (p. 147) we consider how best to research this information, but one thing that it is important to point out here is that much of it will come from sources that will be less familiar to you than the traditional textbooks and websites you have used previously for AS Media Studies.

As you can see, we also suggest that you might go to some primary sources for information. Getting notes from such sources is a different kind of challenge from researching material from books and websites. The skills in doing this are closely allied to those of a journalist or a media researcher collecting qualitative data. You may wish to consider asking the person you are interviewing if you can record the interview so that you can play it back later. Your mobile could have a facility to allow you to do this. Above all be sure you are properly prepared for the interview. In essence this means having an interview strategy planned, usually in the form of questions that you intend to ask. Don't forget that it is better to adopt a flexible approach to the interview rather than to mechanistically ask your questions regardless of the response you are getting. As long as you stick to your basic strategy you should be prepared to pursue some of the more interesting issues and ideas raised by the interviewee.

Once you have established that you have all the notes you need, your second job is to organise them into a user-friendly system. One way to do this is according to exam topic. Some of your notes may go under a general heading. This might include for example some of the major theories that you feel you must know. Other sections could be centred around the topics you intend to tackle. So, you may have a section on new/digital media or audience and identity. In the case of new media this might include an overview of the topic, perhaps organised into sections such as:

- Interactive audiences
- The internet
- Globalisation and new media
- Cross-cultural factors and the use/effects of new media technology.

Much of the remainder of your notes in this section could be organised around the exemplification of the ideas contained in the section. You might also consider using the headings from the specification, which as you will have read indicate the areas where questions may be asked. So a heading which deals with, say, the changing contemporary media landscape would be especially useful in revising this potential exam topic area.

If you organise your notes along these lines, they should both make sense and be easy to navigate. Spending time looking through notes and then finding they make no sense is a complete waste of time.

Study skills

Activity

In the AS section of this book, we asked students to look at their notes and on the basis of that evidence to place themselves on a scale of 1 to 10 for adjectives that might best describe their approach to study. It may be a good idea to have a go at the same activity one year later. Here it is:

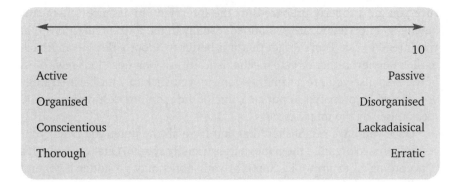

1	10
Active	Passive
Organised	Disorganised
Conscientious	Lackadaisical
Thorough	Erratic

So how did you score this time? Of course the ideal is lots of low numbers. Realistically you would be pretty bad company if you really do live such a virtuous life. However, you might be pretty bad company if you are scoring tens constantly. Most of you will be scoring an average of somewhere in the middle.

You can use this as the basis for a SWOT analysis. SWOT stands for Strengths, Weaknesses, Opportunities and Threats. As you may have guessed it is a bit of management-speak, but it can be useful to you as a Media Studies student. Knowing what your strengths and weaknesses are in terms of exam performance is going to be helpful to you in your preparation for the coming exams. You should also make yourself aware of what opportunities present themselves in the run-up to your exam. For example, the chance to visit a media organisation might be an opportunity to be grasped with both hands. Probably the biggest threat to your achievement is your own inability to knuckle down to the task ahead.

One place that you could very usefully start your SWOT analysis is with your AS exams and any mock exams that you have done for A2. For each of these it is worth making an appraisal along the following lines:

1   What did I achieve?
2   Was I surprised by my achievement?
3   Did I deserve this achievement?
4   What particular strengths did I take into the exam?
5   If I could do the exam again, what elements of my preparation would I improve on?

The answers to these questions should help you find a strategy for preparing for the A2 exams. Your aim should be to find a means of revising and preparing that will enable you to maximise your achievement. The last question is the one that needs most focus. As an A2 student you have already had the benefit of experiencing at least one set of Media Studies exams. Learn from the experience of doing these. Try to write a list of three or four points where you think you might be better prepared this time. For example, you may feel that you went into the exam a bit light on good examples of products for the case study section. When you come to take MEST3, make sure you get it right this time.

Planning your revision

Another skill you should be developing is that of time management. At A2 the pressure is on, or at least it should be. Media Studies exams will be just one of the many demands on your time. The hours that you are able to devote to it are precious, so you must use them wisely.

One thing you will almost certainly know well in advance is the dates of your exams. You should have learned from your previous studies that taking a long run at your exams is likely to have much better impact on your results than a last-minute sprint. This means that you need to plan your revision. Let's assume that you decide to start revising in earnest for your MEST3 exam a couple of months before they are due. That means that you have roughly 60 days to get yourself ready. How are you going to use these 60 days? Well, of course you won't really have 60 days. There will be lots of other things to fill your time but you should try to give up between one and two hours a day for your A2 revision. So that means an average of about 90 hours for the two exams.

If you think about the two sections, A and B, it should be apparent to you that there is rather more you can do in the way of revision for Section B than for Section A. The very nature of an unseen exam question tends to limit the amount of revision that's possible. That does not of course mean that you don't do any – far from it! What it does means is that the balance of time that you spend between the two exams should favour Section B, which demands more specific revision than Section A. You need therefore to arrive at a compromise which would give the following balance of hours:

MEST3 Section A – 30 hours
MEST3 Section B – 60 hours

You need to bear in mind that Section B is worth more marks than Section A, and therefore you should spend a little more time on revising for that section. Section A is worth 32 marks and Section B is worth 48 marks in total.

This is not a hard and fast rule. It may be you want to shift the balance one way or another. That is for you to decide. You may even feel that the amount of hours suggested is far too many or far too few. Again that is for you to decide. The important issue here is that you spend at least some time revising and that the time you allocate is properly organised and spent wisely. Revision that is random is very difficult to sustain and usually quite unproductive.

> Don't forget about the therapeutic power of lists. Whenever possible write down a list of things you have to do as part of your revision programme. Your list can be either a short focused list of your revision topics or an epic list of things to do with your life more generally, including A2 Media Studies revision topics. Lists help you organise. More importantly they help you prioritise. One feature of being stressed is that you lose all sense of the amount of time a task might take or how difficult it might be. Every task seems like a mountain to climb.

Once you have a list, try numbering the order you intend to do the items in. Group together tasks that you can undertake in the same location – for example, the library. Try to build in some contrasts in the list – for example, different activities or different topics, so that there is a variety in what you do. This helps stave off the boredom factor.

The therapy comes as you are able to feel the warm inner glow of crossing off items on the list until you finally get to the last one. Think then of the reward you have promised yourself for such virtuous dedication to your revision programme.

Later in this part in the sections on MEST3 Sections A and B we give details on how you should go about preparing for these exams. You may find it a useful thought to consider now what kind of organisational strategies you are going to adopt for your revision plan. Let's try to get you started.

Section B of the exam requires you to answer one from a choice of four questions, two from each of the two pre-set topics. Unless you are a super conscientious student you will have prepared just two case studies for this paper, one for each topic. Given that you have a global figure of 60 hours to use for revision, logically you will split this time between the two topics, that is, 30 hours each. Of course you may feel that one topic needs more attention than the other. Perhaps you have focused heavily on one topic, such as news, for your Critical Investigation coursework unit and, therefore, feel more confident about it than the other topic. No problem here about adjusting the number of hours as long as you don't get blasé about it.

Important information about the MEST3 pre-set topics can be found on p. 141. Make sure you know exactly what the topics are that are being tested in the exam you take. If you have any doubt, ask your teacher.

NOTE

So how are you going to use these 30 hours for your topic? Well, we can break it down into some of its constituent parts. These might include:

- *Core concepts*. You can find these as bullet points which form the content of each topic area in the specification. There are usually between four and six bullet points to cover.
- *Products*. You need to look in detail at media products that you can use to exemplify the concepts you have identified above.
- *Contexts*. This is potentially time-consuming if you have not done the research as you go along. If you have, then it is a matter of reading around the contexts in which the products you have explored were produced. Of course, you then need to make links with these contexts, the products and the concepts.
- *Theory*. You need to feel confident that you know and can apply some of the key theories to all the above.
- *Issues and debates*. You need to be able to discuss the wider media issues and debates which are relevant to your case studies and the overall topic.

Use these five headings as the basis of your revision checklist for each of the case studies for the two topics. You may want to allocate an equal amount of time to each. That is unlikely. Much more probable is that you will want to consider each in turn and prioritise them according to how much time you think each would benefit from. For instance, if you think theory is your weak area, then not only might this get a big slice of the 30 hours, it might also be the place you start your revision.

Activity

Use the ideas and information above to help you draw up a revision plan for each of the MEST3 case studies. This plan should enable you to make the most effective use of the hours you intend to allocate for this unit. At this stage try to get a broad overview of what it is you need to confront in this unit. The fine-tuning and detail can be added when we have sorted out your approach to MEST3 Section A.

MEST3 Section A revision poses a series of interesting challenges. Potentially this is the most demanding area of assessment for the whole AQA Media Studies A level qualification. As you will read in the section on Section A, we are looking at more than analysis here. You may think that writing about an unseen product, as you did at AS, is in itself hard enough but in MEST3 we are looking at two products and we need to add some details about contexts, theories, issues and debates. So where can you start revising for that sort of exam?

Well, it would be foolish to pretend it is easy. MEST3 Section A by its very nature is a voyage into the unknown. The only predictable element is that about six weeks before you take the exam, your teacher should be able to tell you if there is going to be a moving image product included. Even if there is a moving image product indicated, they still won't be able to tell you whether there will be one such product or two.

Preparing for MEST3 Section A is about getting yourself ready to respond to whatever is placed in front of you. Section A of the exam is probably the ultimate test of your ability to apply your conceptual understanding of the discipline of Media Studies. So one thing that you need to make sure that you are up to speed on is the key concepts which played such a large part in your preparation for the AS exams. You should by now know exactly what they are, but just in case here they are again:

- Media Representations
- Media Language
- Media Institutions
- Media Values and Ideology
- Media Audiences.

One strategy for revision is to practise applying these key concepts to any media product you come across in much the same way you did in preparing for the AS exam. You can do this formally by looking closely at a product and writing notes under the key concept headings. Alternatively you can do it informally by mentally applying the concepts to products that you encounter in your daily routine. Billboards you see on the way to school or college offer a rich opportunity for this type of activity.

The next step is to start looking for similarities in the products you encounter. Obviously there will be similarities between products in terms of genre and media form, but also look at issues of intertextuality where products might relate to one another in slightly different ways – for example, the relationship between a billboard advertisement and a television or magazine advertisement for the same product. Try to make some notes on how the two relate in terms of points of comparison. You might like to start at a fairly basic level by considering their similarities and differences. Have the key concepts handy to guide you on this. Issues of representation, for example, can be an interesting focus point – do the two products represent the same thing in different ways or in very similar ways? Similarly, get used to comparing the media language of different products – for example, how each one uses narrative to communicate to the audience. Any mention of audience should immediately get you thinking around that key concept. You may consider the different ways in which the products address their audiences and what assumptions each product makes about its audience.

Being able to respond quickly to these kinds of cues is an important skill if you are going to do well in the MEST3 exam. Remember that this is baseline stuff, just a little way on from what you did in the AS exam. By now it should almost be second nature to reach for your analytical toolkit whenever a product or pair of products captures your interest.

Activity

Whenever you become interested in an individual product, start thinking about other products that you might link it to. Put yourself in the position of the principal examiner for MEST3 and try to identify products that form interesting pairings. Do this across media forms as well. Think about how, for example, a moving image product might relate to a print product covering a similar topic or theme.

As you will realise from your reading of the MEST3 Section A material, this kind of comparative analysis is very much a starting point in the exam, not an end point. As you will be aware, two important issues are the linking of wider contexts and theoretical perspectives. You should see the latter in revision terms as an extension of your application of the key concepts to the products. By the time you have reached the revision stage you should have at least a nodding acquaintance with some of the key theoretical perspectives. Ideally you should be on first name terms with a good many of them. So get used to looking at individual products and, better still, pairs of products to see what theoretical perspective you think might be applied.

Getting your head around contexts for Section A is much more demanding. There is clearly going to be some element of luck in the products that turn up in the exam even though on the exam paper itself you will be given some background information about each of the products. You may or may not already know something of the background to the products that you are looking at. However, detailed historical knowledge about the background is not part of the mark scheme. Use the information supplied on the paper wisely and then learn to read into the wider contexts via the products themselves. Of course, some basic grasp of politics and recent history will help you here, so part of the way into revising wider contexts is through your own intellectual curiosity. Being aware of issues by doing simple things such as reading the *Guardian*'s media supplement the 'Media Guardian' and taking an interest in 'serious' news will help you a lot here. Don't forget that you may have notes from other GCE subjects that could add to your broader knowledge of social and cultural contexts. History and Sociology are two subjects that might help. When you are confronted with a non-contemporary product, try to get some detail of the background. This is a skill you should have developed for both Section B of the exam and your coursework.

Try adding this contextual dimension to the product that you have looked at previously. Learn to move beyond the product into the broader social and cultural issues that it raises. Focus for example on some of the ethical issues that certain media output might raise. Confessional television shows and newspaper 'exposés' of the private lives of celebrities all provide opportunities to rehearse a multitude of issues relating to media ethics.

Revising for MEST3 Section A is about learning to identify and exploit opportunities. Practise this both mentally and more formally by choosing pairs of products and writing an essay response in note form. You will be surprised how accomplished you can become at this.

In contrast to this, you exert much more control over your preparation for MEST3 Section B since you have shaped and conducted your case studies yourself. Up to the time you are revising with the examination firmly in your sights, less of your lesson time devoted to Section B is likely to have been led by your teacher in a conventional teaching scenario with you making notes and participating in a variety of activities designed to help you learn the key skills, theories and concepts. Instead, research and independent study will have formed the basis of the preparation which, if you have taken notice of our advice to be an active rather than a passive student, you will have been able to do successfully.

And so your revision, such as it is, will be based upon familiarising yourself with the results of the research you have undertaken, being very familiar with the media products which form the backbone of the studies and the associated secondary research into the work of authors, theorists, academics and media professionals and, crucially, practising answers by attempting past questions and having them marked by your teachers.

Creating a plan – being prepared to modify it

So you should have by now some idea of the task that is confronting you. The next thing to do is to create a plan. With any luck this is something you are used to doing after your experience of revision for AS Media Studies and your other AS exams. The best way to achieve this is by using a big wall planner or the calendar on your computer, which has the delightfully irritating habit of reminding you on a hourly basis what you have to do.

Try to plan your revision to give yourself some variety. Also look at links between revision for the two sections of MEST3. Certainly some of the theoretical information and the wider contexts may well overlap to save you time. Don't forget that watching a DVD or reading a magazine can count towards your revision providing you focus on their possible value as exemplars in an exam answer or preparation for unseen products in MEST3 Section A.

Remember too that your plan is a guide, not a binding contract. Don't ever let the plan become too much for you. Be prepared to trim it where necessary if you feel you are falling behind. Be prepared to prioritise, paying attention to those areas that most need it.

How and where to revise

You should by this stage have a clear sense of what is the most effective way for you to revise. If you have a system that works, then skip this section and get on with some revision. If you still find it hard to get on with revision, then you may find some of the ideas below helpful.

You should really know by now what works best for you when it comes to the logistics of revision. If you don't, then it is about time you found out. Here are some ideas that you might like to consider to help you. One thing you might find useful is go back to some advice we offered for your AS revision so that you can consider just where your time goes.

It is important to remember that everyone is different. Consequently there are no hard and fast rules for how best to revise. What matters most is that you find out for yourself a method of revising that is going to be the most effective. You also need to find out a method of revising that makes optimum use of your precious time. Again this means getting organised. It is quite a salutary experience to make an analysis of how you spend your time over a period of a week, broken down in terms of the 168 available hours. A fairly rough breakdown will do. It can be realised in terms of activities such as:

- sleeping
- leisure activities
- working (as in paid employment)
- travelling
- study (in and out of class).

First, you need to think what has worked best so far. It is probably not a good idea to start trying out new revision strategies close to one of the most important exams you are likely to take. Think back to your most recent experience of exam revision. For most people this is likely to be the AS exam less than a year ago. You may also want to think back a little further to how you tackled your GCSE revision. One thing you probably noticed is that there is quite a significant difference in demand between GCSE and AS. You may also have noticed that AS calls for rather different skills.

Use the questions below to help you focus on how you went about AS revision, and what was good and what was not so good about your approach.

Noise. Just how sensitive are you to noise as a source of distraction?

Very sensitive ☐
Oblivious ☐

Hell is other people. How helpful do you find it to be supported by other people?

Helpful ☐
Really irritated by them ☐

Do you work best on your own or as part of a group of people revising together?

Love groups ☐
Hate groups ☐

Attention span. Different people have different attention spans. What is your optimum attention span? Do you start to flag after half an hour and need to do something else for a short while to get your concentration and motivation back? Or can you keep going for a couple of hours especially with the promise of a reward at the end?

Can concentrate for hours ☐
Ten minutes max ☐

Where is the best place to work to ensure you have access to everything that you need? Remember you may need to use a computer and text-books as well as your notes.

Bedroom ☐
Town centre ☐

Can you get anything useful done in short bursts – for example, on short journeys or during breaks? It is a good idea to make sure you always have something useful to hand such as a textbook when opportunities for short bursts of revision arise.

Yes   ❑

No   ❑

The answers to these questions should help you with your revision focus. Use them to optimise the conditions under which you revise. If you arrive at the conclusion that your best revision strategy is to work alone in your bedroom with a computer in complete silence for a maximum of an hour, then try to create these ideal conditions. For example, wait until the rest of the household have gone out or are in bed if quietness is a real imperative for you. Above all be prepared to be flexible. It may be that the only place you can find to work is with your laptop on the bus home with a set of earplugs in place. Life is never quite as you would like it to be.

MEST4: how it can help

Believe it or not, when qualifications such as GCE Media Studies are designed, there is a logic that informs both individual units and the relationship between them. By this stage in the course you may well have completed your MEST4 coursework, comprising the independent study and the practical production. If you have, then this is a good time to look back at what you did and think about how it might help you prepare for the upcoming MEST3 exam. Alternatively, if you are still in the process of completing MEST4, it is probably an even better opportunity to do this. Either way it is important to realise that both units were designed with a similar ethos in mind and that you can use your experience of the MEST4 unit to ensure you are on track with MEST3. In essence the link is that both units enjoy a common approach to the way in which you are encouraged to learn and the skills that you are developing. Let's have a look at how.

As part of the process of completing your MEST4 independent study, you should have looked in some detail and depth at quite a range of different products. The analytical skills you developed in this exploration are precisely the same skills you need to apply in both sections of the MEST3 exam. Furthermore, some of your analysis is likely to have been comparative in the sense that you will have looked at more than one product and drawn some comparison and considered them in light of one another. Make sure you use these skills specifically in relation to Section A of MEST4. Indeed if you are still actively engaged in preparing your MEST4 independent study, use it as an opportunity to hone your skills in looking at two products in relation to each other. The simple process of finding products that work together as 'pairs' of the sort you may encounter in MEST3 Section A is in itself a valuable activity in preparing for the exam.

MEST4 should also have taught you the importance of seeing media products within a much wider context than your own consumption or preparation for the exam. For both MEST3 and MEST4 you need to ask the question: what makes a media product the way it is? The answer may well be quite complex as you are potentially exploring the economic, cultural, social and political influences that are at play in media production. You can, however, simplify your take on contexts by looking at:

- The forces that impact on the production of products – for example, the effects of technology on the way in which media products are created and distributed.
- The contexts in which media products are consumed and the ways in which audiences use and take pleasure from the media they encounter.

THE NEXT STEP: REVISION AND EXAM PLANNING

Hopefully the fact that you are now armed with a realistic revision plan, based on a recognition of how much time you need to revise and the conditions you need to work in successfully, has made you feel more in control of the process of exam preparation, and therefore calm. At this point you need to embark on the content-specific work – analysing media products, reviewing and clarifying your case study in the context of exam questions and assessment. In the following sections you will find reminders of the media key concepts, examples of successful case studies and exam essay activities to support your own work. Good luck!

MEST3 CRITICAL PERSPECTIVES SECTION A

Assessment at a glance: Section A

- This section will test your understanding of:

    - Media concepts
    - Wider contexts
    - Media issues and debates.

- Section A is worth 32 marks, 40% of the total for the exam.
- You should spend 1 hour on this (including 15 minutes reading/viewing time).
- You will need to spend time making notes and planning your answers.
- You will be given unseen stimulus materials.
- The unseen materials and questions will be linked to the MEST3 topic areas.
- You will need to answer 3 compulsory questions on the materials.
- Your answers will be in short essay-style format.
- Your answers for questions 2 and 3 should include examples from your study of the media, including the case studies which you have prepared for Section B of MEST3.
- Section A assesses AO1 which is the ability to 'demonstrate knowledge and understanding of media concepts, contexts and critical debates' (AQA specification).

What is Critical Perspectives Section A about?

MEST3 is based on the study of two pre-set topics. For students taking the exam in June 2014 these topics are:

- The impact of new/digital media
- Representations in the media.

For students entering for the exam from June 2015 onwards the topics are:

- The impact of new/digital media
- A topic relating to audience and identity.

The questions will require you to show the knowledge and understanding that you have acquired in your study of the topics, as well as from your AS

MEST3 topics are subject to change. You can get up-to-date information either from your teacher or by visiting the AQA website.

Media Studies course. This is a synoptic paper, meaning that it is intended to test everything you have covered in your course. It is intended to allow you to draw together all the strands of your learning over the two years. In some respects this exam can seem to be quite a challenge, as it requires you to apply a huge range of learning from both years of your A level, as well as drawing on your wider knowledge from beyond the classroom. In addition to this, you will have no prior knowledge of the actual products, beyond knowing whether they are moving image or not. As a consequence, this part of the exam can seem particularly stressful, as there are so many 'unknowns'. We hope that this section will prove to you that actually there is much you can do to reduce any anxiety, especially if, first, you understand what the exam is expecting of you. Second, there is plenty you can do to prepare for this exam in terms of targeting your revision wisely and making sure that you have practised answering the different types of questions in this section.

The key to success is understanding the nature of the exam and making sure that you understand the mind of the examiner. What are they looking for? What makes a good answer? How can you improve the quality of your answers? How much to write? What style of answer is appropriate? What types of examples should you use? How should you use the time available in the exam? What preparation can you do beforehand? This section aims to break down this part of the exam in order to answer these questions and ensure that you have every opportunity to succeed.

Section A is based on your response to two 'unseen' media products. You will be asked three questions, which require short answer questions. You will be given time to make notes and plan your response to the two unseen products. The first question will be on the two products, but you will need to refer to other media products in your answers to the other two questions, especially question 3. The questions will link into the topic areas you have prepared for MEST3.

Even though you may panic at the thought of the unseen products, there is much you can do to prepare for this part of the exam. Your performance in the exam relies a lot on exam technique – understanding how to use the time, making notes and identifying what the question is asking for. You should aim to use your lessons and teacher input as the start of your preparation for this part of the exam, and try to practise and prepare as much as possible in your own time. The earlier you do this the better.

What is meant by 'Critical Perspectives'?

This exam is entitled 'Critical Perspectives' as it is all about the 'bigger picture' surrounding media products. This is a big step up from AS Media Studies, which is more limited in terms of the frame of reference you are expected to employ. A2 Media Studies is about your broader knowledge and understanding – essentially what does the product tell us about the media industry and society as a whole? What influences have moulded its production, and what debates arise from the product? This exam paper is all about you applying appropriate critical frameworks in developing different *perspectives* – views or insights – on the products. These *critical* frameworks consist of different theories, debates, issues and concepts.

Revision tip

Read broadsheet newspapers and look out for stories about the media. What issues and debates are raised by the stories? What products are mentioned? Make notes on what the stories tell you about trends and debates in the media industry. Think about their relevance to your case study topics: audience and identity; the impact of new media technology.

The *Guardian* website has a whole section devoted to the media where you can research your case studies further and find out what is happening in the media world.

The two topics for MEST3 are chosen as a focus for your consideration of media products, although the scope for your answers will be much wider than that. For example the two current topics – audience and identity and the impact of new/digital media – both provoke debates and issues which are at the heart of contemporary Media Studies. Your consumption of the media, both in and out of the classroom, will provide you with many examples of products which you can discuss in questions 2 and 3. When watching a film you could consider issues concerning audience and identity for example, or consider how issues surrounding new media have an impact when using social networking media or playing a new computer game. These topic areas will be implicit in your everyday media consumption, you just need to be alert to them, and making notes on a regular basis.

Activity

As part of your revision you should keep a media diary, focusing on examples of media products and how they are relevant to the topic areas. Make notes on any relevant news stories – for example, the negative effects of new media technology. By making notes you will be thinking about your topic areas, which will help reinforce your learning.

Below is a list of critical perspectives you will need for MEST3.

Media concepts

In developing your discussion of the products, you will need to demonstrate your understanding of media concepts. These should all be familiar to you from having studied AS Media Studies.

You are being tested on:

- Form (media language)
- Narrative
- Genre
- Representations
- Institution
- Audience
- Values

Revision tip

Remember to revise your AS notes regarding media concepts as this will be fundamental to answering Question 1. You must be confident and secure in writing about the key concepts. Question 1 at A2 is different from the AS exam in that it will require you to focus on one media concept rather than all of them.

media industry
The organisations which are behind the production, marketing, distribution and regulation of media products.

media production
The process, including financial implications, involved in creating a media product.

distribution
The marketing and advertising of a media product.

exhibition
Where, when and how a product is consumed by its audience.

Media industry

You must be prepared to consider media products in terms of the bigger picture of the role and form of the media in today's society. The paper will be examining your understanding of the media institutions and how they operate within the media industry as a whole, in particular:

- media production
- distribution
- exhibition.

What does it mean to consider the industrial context? Let's think about how this works with a specific product: the BBC detective series *Sherlock*, starring Benedict Cumberbatch and Martin Freeman.

Figure 9
DVD cover for *Sherlock Holmes*.

Activity

- How is this product typical of the BBC?
- What are the main issues and debates concerning the BBC in contemporary broadcasting?
- How does the industrial context of *Sherlock* compare with other products you have studied?

The following points could be made about the industrial context for the series:

- Relatively high-budget drama targeting a more sophisticated middle-class demographic.
- BBC brand image of high-quality drama – BBC has a reputation for similar series such as *Dr Who*, an iconic BBC product which defines the BBC's established brand image, having first been broadcast fifty years ago.
- Co-production between the British-based Hartswood Films and American public service television provider WGBH – demonstrates the trend towards transnational co-productions, which allows for a bigger budget and therefore greater chance of marketing product globally.
- High-production values enhancing appeal to a global audience: distinguished cast, special effects.
- Sold to over 150 different global broadcasters – success has resulted in two series, with a third planned for the future.
- BBC competing with global media conglomerates – global nature of contemporary broadcasting.
- Distinctively British content, cast and production team.
- *Dr Who* production team involvement – building on success of the *Dr Who* franchise in recent years – another successful BBC export.
- Adaptation of literary classic helps satisfy BBC's commitment to public service broadcasting, and helps promote a brand image of quality and Britishness.
- Marketing campaign made use of dedicated websites which tie in to the narrative of the series.
- Third series in the making resulting from global success and star status of central actors: Martin Freeman taking leading role in *The Hobbit*, Benedict Cumberbatch to star in the next *Star Trek* movie.
- Income from overseas sales helps subsidise the income of the BBC, which is largely reliant on the licence fee (which has been frozen in recent years).

- Each episode is the length of a feature film, reflecting its status of having a high budget and high production values.
- Quirky visual style updating the literary classic – competing with other contemporary adaptations, in particular the Robert Downey, Jr. films.
- Continuing reliance on remakes and adaptations in both film and television: aversion to risk-taking within the media industry, especially given the size of the budgets involved.

A discussion of the industrial context draws on many possible aspects of the product, encompassing media language, audience, values, new technology and the impact of globalisation in this particular case. It involves a consideration of how the product is typical of the television industry, and in particular the British television industry and the BBC. You should note the transmedia issues that are relevant to the discussion of industry. The BBC used the internet to help promote the programme for example, and the film industry is also relevant to the discussion, with the star status of the lead actors beyond television, and the film adaptations of the Sherlock Holmes stories. This is key to the synoptic approach which is required by MEST3.

Activity

Make notes about the industrial context for the media products you have covered for your case study. What does this tell you about the relationship between the media producers, their audiences and the products themselves? Are your products typical of the media industry? Are there any noticeable trends or issues? Are there any unusual products you have come across in terms of how they have been produced, distributed and exhibited?

WIDER CONTEXTS

You need to consider this industrial context and the products themselves in the light of wider contexts, specifically:

- social
- political
- historical
- economic.

Let's think about how this could work with our case study of *Sherlock*. Even though *Sherlock* is based on the original Conan Doyle stories, it has

social context
What does the product tell you in terms of broader social issues and debates? Can you identify any broader context in terms of what it says about the society which produced and consumes the product?

political context
Does the product have a political message? Certain products might have more overt political messages such as documentaries or news products, whereas others might have a more implicit message.

historical context
Is the product a contemporary one? If not, what does it tell you about the society, values and media of its time? Does it represent a particular historical period? If so, what can you say about the representation?

economic context
This crosses over with the industrial context in terms of a focus on the funding and business context of the product. Debates about the media industry, its organisation, regulation and globalisation are all relevant here.

adapted and updated them to reflect contemporary social concerns. Certain themes are repeated throughout the series such as a concern about the inadequacy of the police when faced with serious crime, a distrust of the authorities, in particular politicians and the government, offering potential for discussing the political context. These themes provide a background for stories which deal with terrorism, the impact of modern technology and the military.

In terms of social context, you could also consider *Sherlock* from the point of view of gender roles. The series has been criticised for perpetuating gender stereotypes, as the central characters (Sherlock Holmes, Dr Watson, Moriarty and Detective Inspector Lestrade) are male whereas the few female characters tend to provide only comic relief (as with the ditsy landlady Mrs Hudson) or sex appeal on the whole. This discussion could be developed further to compare the BBC's *Sherlock* to other contemporary adaptations, including the Robert Downey, Jr. Sherlock Holmes films and *Elementary* (which stars Lucy Liu as Dr Watson). The BBC adaptation also plays with gender roles, developing an ambiguous relationship between Sherlock and Watson. The representation of masculinity is not straightforward, combining traditional gender traits with more stereotypically feminine traits.

Even though *Sherlock* is a contemporary adaptation, it could be useful for discussing the historical context of the series, in terms of its debt to the original stories which are set in Victorian and Edwardian Britain. The series represents London in particular as a dark and crime-ridden place, where the government and authorities cannot be trusted. This is made evident in the visual style of the series, which is dominated by low-key lighting and desaturated colours, creating a sinister but exciting setting. Good can only overcome evil as a result of the freakish genius of the individual, with the help of friendship.

Media issues and debates

Question 2 will focus on a particular issue or debate which is relevant to contemporary media products.

Examples of these may include:

- the impact of new media technologies
- media controversies
- concern about media and audiences
- alternative media forms
- power and the media
- audience interaction with the media
- media and its place in society

- audience pleasure and the media
- regulation and the media
- globalisation
- representations and stereotypes
- intertextuality.

The issue or debate will always arise out of the media products you are given. Past examples have covered the use of shock tactics, the use of conflict in the media, the appeal of the 'outsider' to media audiences and regulation of the internet. The questions tend to focus on the relationship between the audience and the media, touching on the use of specific techniques, representations or tactics to reach target audiences. In discussing the relevant issue or debate you will need to consider how it is employed in the 'unseen' products, and then how it is typical of the media as a whole, perhaps using other examples of products that are comparable to, or maybe even contrast with, your exam products.

Media theories

You will need to apply relevant theories to the products to develop discussion of the issues and debates. Your answers to any of the three questions may involve drawing on relevant theory in order to develop the sophistication of your response. The theories you may have covered that might be useful may include:

- genre
- narrative – for example, Barthes, Vogler, Levi-Strauss, Todorov
- analysis – for example, semiotics
- audience – for example, uses and gratifications, effects models, audience pleasures, interactive, Dyer's utopian pleasures
- critical perspectives – for example, Marxist, feminist, queer, postmodern and postcolonial theories.

This is clearly not an exhaustive list, but it would be useful for you to revise the key theories you have covered. Don't worry about what you haven't covered; the key to exam success is how you apply what you have covered.

It is important that you are able to demonstrate your ability to use theory appropriately, and not to merely list theories without applying them to the products. By applying relevant theories you can demonstrate your understanding of key arguments and perspectives regarding media products. It is important that you refer to appropriate theories in a meaningful way by explaining their relevance to the products and questions. For example, rather than just writing:

> The advert uses Barthes' enigma codes.

you should develop your point further to explain how and why, considering how it is typical of advertising conventions and how this appeals to the audience. For example:

> The advert uses Barthes' enigma codes through its use of fast-paced editing and puzzling imagery. The advertiser is seeking to involve the audience more actively in the text, as they try to make sense of the imagery and message and will therefore pay more attention when the advert is shown again.

The exam board clearly states that you are not expected to learn all media theories (an impossible task!), but that you should 'be able to use elements of relevant media theories when analysing media texts'. The theories they list in the specification are suggested as being useful, but are certainly not compulsory.

WIDER CONTEXTS

Question 3 will require you to move beyond the unseen products to consider wider contexts concerning the media. The type of question you will come across will involve consideration of areas such as the following:

- How are the products typical of the media industry?
- What trends and changes are evident that can be found in other products?
- What do the products suggest in terms of social issues and debates?
- What political implications or issues are raised by the products?
- What economic issues are suggested by the products in terms of the contemporary media industry?

Past questions have involved discussion of contemporary topics such as the use of online marketing to target audiences and regulation of the media. With the *Sherlock* case study we were developing points to consider the wider context all the time. This exam is not just about the products themselves but about what the products show us about the media as a whole – whether that is in terms of concepts, debates, issues, theories or overall trends. This is how you should be thinking about media products – in what way are they *typical*?

What will the paper look like?

The front page of the exam booklet contains a lot of important information, which many students ignore in their hurry to get to the questions. Make sure that you read this information carefully, as it will remind you what to do and how to do it. Spend time looking at the past papers on the website to familiarise yourself with the instructions and layout of the paper.

The front cover will tell you:

- *Time allowed* (2 hours for the whole paper – Sections A and B, including 15 minutes viewing time)
- *Instructions* on which questions to answer and how to use the space in the answer booklet
- *Information* regarding marking
- *Advice* on how to use the time.

The *instructions* will remind you to write the questions in the space provided. It is important that you get the examiner on your side by following instructions, and not creating a problem for them when it comes to marking your answers.

The *information* regarding marking will remind you that you will be marked on your written English skills, specifically:

- use good English
- organise relevant information clearly
- use specialist vocabulary where appropriate.

You clearly need to write accurately and fluently, use appropriate media terminology and organise your answers appropriately. Not only does this help the examiner to read your answer, but it will also help your mark. Your use of media terminology will demonstrate your knowledge and under-standing of the subject as well.

The front cover will remind you of the *assessment criteria*: your knowl-edge and understanding of:

- media concepts, contexts and critical debates
- how meanings and responses are created within media products and processes.

Questions 2 and 3 will indicate that you can refer to other media products which are relevant to the question. This is particularly important with ques-tion 3, which asks that you 'should refer to other media products to support your answer'.

You can look at all the past papers on the AQA website.

http://web.aqa.org.uk/qual/gce/media-studies/media-studies-materials.php

All the past papers have consisted of *two* previously unseen media products. These could be from any form of media: print, moving image, audio or website. There will be a clear linking theme between the products in terms of media concepts, wider contexts and media debates. This linking theme will tie in with the *topic areas* for MEST3, and will therefore draw on your knowledge and understanding acquired during the year.

What to expect: the unseen products

It may well be that you are unfamiliar with the products, but do not let that be a problem. You need to be aware that the products will have been chosen because of the issues, debates and wider contextual factors that arise from them. The products tend to be topical ones, which will raise issues that you will have studied as part of your preparation for the case studies for MEST3. Use the information you have been given on the exam paper about the products to focus on relevant issues and contextual factors in preparation for note-making.

If you are familiar with the products, you may well feel that you have hit the jackpot and that the exam is in the bag. Unfortunately not so! You must remain focused on the question, and not be tempted to write everything you know about the product. You are rewarded for applying your media knowledge and understanding, not for detailed description of the product.

NOTE

The term 'product' implies the approach you should take in this exam. A product implies an industrial process, which opens up debates and issues surrounding the media industry. In this respect you need to consider:

- Who produced the product?
- Who was the product produced for?
- What are the implications in terms of regulation?
- What is the purpose of the product?
- What implications are there as far as technology are concerned?
- How does the product reflect the values and ideologies of the society within which it is produced?

The types of products you will receive will be in the following formats:

1   *Print products*, which will be included as part of the exam paper issued to you. They will be produced in the form of an insert or additional sheet

folded into your paper. They could take the form of an advertisement, film poster or an extract from a newspaper or magazine. You will still have note-making time, and will have the products in front of you throughout the exam.

2 *Moving image products* in the form of a DVD which will be played to you three times in order to give you the opportunity to study it thoroughly before writing your answer. This may take a variety of forms including a television advertisement, a film or television programme trailer or the opening sequence of a programme. Your note-taking skills will be critical in making sure that you make the best use of the viewing time at the start of the exam. You will not be able to go back to the products to check details, and will have to rely on your notes for your answers.

3 *E-media products* which may take the form of a printout of a website for example, or perhaps a DVD presentation of a YouTube video.

4 *Another media format* such as a radio extract is also possible. (So far there has been no use of this format in the exam, but it is listed as a possibility in the specification.)

Remember you are given two products, and it is conceivable that you could be given a mixture of two formats – for example, a print product and a moving image product –although at the time of publication this has not been the case so far.

The unseen products: making links

The two unseen products will be linked in some way which will relate to the question areas. Past papers have used pairings of products which are linked by:

* subject matter
* form
* genre
* representations
* issues and debates.

These are just examples of how the products can be linked. The June 2011 exam featured the Adidas House Party advert and two NHS/government adverts to warn young people of the dangers of excess alcohol. The products provide a clear starting point for comparison; for instance, they both featured representations of young people partying. Both products were targeting a youth audience and making use of digital platforms to do this. As you can see there will be clear links across the two products, but you should also expect differences which will help you develop a debate in your answers. The two advertising campaigns used very different tactics to reach their audiences, having very different objectives. The NHS adverts used shock tactics in order to warn the youth audience, whereas the Adidas campaign used celebrities to attract attention and endorse the brand.

Activity

Watch the adverts mentioned above and make a list of any other differences and similarities across the products. What other products can you link these campaigns with in terms of the differences/similarities you have uncovered?
You can find the adverts online:

Adidas House Party: http://vimeo.com/8183564
NHS Know Your Limits:
www.youtube.com/watch?v=zkVqJTK0ioc&feature=

By considering the links across the products you should be able to come up with ideas for comparable products in terms of the key similarities and differences.

Activity

1   List the products you have studied for MEST3. Can you pair them up in any way? Consider form, representations, issues, subject matter and key debates. What other products are comparable?
2   List your ideas for similarities and differences between the following:

  •   BBC's *Sherlock* and Channel 4 US import *The Killing*.
  •   Front covers of the *Sun* and website for the *Guardian* for the same day.
  •   Front cover of *Men's Health* magazine and website for *Attitude*.

For each pairing think of other products which you could refer to in developing your points regarding the similarities and differences.

Using the case studies to prepare for Section A

The unseen products and the three questions for Section A will be based on the topics set for MEST3. This means that you will have already done some preparation for these questions, having covered the concepts, theories, debates and wider contexts relevant to the topics. At the time of writing the two set topics are:

* The impact of new/digital media
* Representations in the media.

One way to approach your revision for these questions is to make a checklist of all the different areas you may have covered for each topic area following the headings suggested by the exam board. For each area list examples from your case study which you could use, thinking about products, debates, issues and theories you may have covered. Let's say you chose to study representations in the media, perhaps starting with reality television and a docusoap, in particular *The Only Way is Essex*.

Activity

To what extent is *The Only Way Is Essex* typical of reality television in terms of representation of identity? (Consider gender, sexuality and regional identity.) What pleasures does reality television offer its audience?

Completing such a chart forces you to summarise your case study under headings which will be the framework behind the choice of the unseen products and questions. Don't worry if you can't complete all the headings – they are only suggestions for areas you might cover, and are not all compulsory. The important thing is that you consider the products you have studied and how you can write about them in answer to the questions. Likewise you need to consider the different aspects of the topic area – theories, debates and wider contexts – and how you can use your products to develop your answers.

Figure 10
Publicity shot for *The Only Way is Essex* series 6.

Table 5 *Example checklist for The Only Way Is Essex*

Representations	Product	Theories, debates and issues
Representations and identity	*The Only Way Is Essex* (*TOWIE*) and other examples of reality TV	Camp/queer theory; feminist theory; post-feminism; representation of social class; representations of regional identity
Genre, representations and audience	*TOWIE*	Docusoaps and representations; genre conventions and audience appeal
Representations and audience positioning	*Made In Chelsea*; *TOWIE*; *Geordie Shore*	Mode of address; demographics/ psychographics and construction of target audiences
Representations, audience pleasures and identity	Range of docusoaps, reality TV and soap operas; gossip magazines; tabloids	Dyer's utopian pleasures; uses and gratifications theory
Cross-media issues	Tabloid/lifestyle magazines: *TOWIE*; use of social networking by music industry e.g. Lady Gaga	Relationship between print/e-media and reality TV; growth of popularity of reality TV; use of internet and digital technologies to engage and involve audience
Issues regarding globalisation and representations	*TOWIE*, *Jersey Shore* etc; *Big Brother*; *I'm A Celebrity*	Global TV formats and regional/national identity
Values and ideologies underlying representations	*TOWIE*; *Educating Essex*; *Made In Chelsea*	Marxist perspective e.g. consumerist values promoted by *TOWIE*

For your second topic, the impact of new/digital media, the framework could look something like the following checklist.

Table 6 *Example of second topic checklist*

Possible areas	Products	Debates/issues
Interactive consumer		
Social networking		
Internet and the world wide web		
Blogs		
Podcasts		
Changing contemporary media landscape		
Role of media institutions		
Media and democracy		
Changing role of distributor and exhibitor		
New technologies and the audience		
Globalisation and new media		
Cross-media factors		
Values and ideology in the impact of new technology		

Again, you need to think about the products you have studied and what debates, issues and theories arose in your lessons. Even if they don't fit perfectly into the chart, just thinking through the topic area and making notes will help you prepare for the exam.

Different learners have different styles of making revision notes which work well for them. You may wish to organise your notes into the form of a mind map for example, with headings for the different topic areas and products.

How to approach Section A questions

The paper will make clear that you:

- MUST answer all *three questions* in Section A
- will be shown moving image/audio products *three times*
- will have time to *make notes* in between each showing
- will have *15 minutes* note-making time if you have print products
- should spend *45 minutes* on Section A.

Section A gives you background information for each of the media products, followed by three questions. The three questions are short-answer questions, requiring an extended paragraph rather than a longer essay length answer as for Section B. The short-answer question is intended to be more focused and to test you on specific concepts, debates and contexts related to the unseen products and the topic areas for MEST3.

Each of the questions will have the number of marks indicated so that you know how much time you should allow. It is really important that you stick to the suggested timings, making sure that you remember not to spend too long on one question at the expense of other questions. It could be easy to feel that you have much more to say in response to one question which is actually worth comparatively few marks. This is a mistake which students make in any exam – so be strict with yourself and remember that timing is crucial.

Section A summary

Question 1: focus on *media concepts* – form, narrative, genre, representation, audience, institution, values; close reference to the two unseen products (8 marks).

> Question 2: *media debates and issues* – based on a media concept (form, narrative, genre, representation, audience, institution, values) but used to explore a media issue/critical debate; close reference to unseen products, but encouraged to refer to other media products (12 marks).
>
> Question 3: *three wider contexts* – you must use wide-ranging examples of other media products in answering this question (12 marks).

We will use the past paper in Figure 11 to demonstrate how this all works in practice.

Planning your answer

The background information is very important. You should read it carefully, as it will help prepare you for making notes on the products and planning your answers. You will be given time to read the paper before the screenings, and should make use of this time to read through the information and questions, highlighting keywords which will help you develop your answers. Using our exemplar paper, we can see that certain keywords indicate what you need to focus on whilst watching the products and making notes.

> Question 1 Evaluate how the two trailers use the *narrative technique of enigma* to encourage the target audience to watch the films.

Looking back at the context set by the information on each product, we can see that we already have some relevant pointers for developing an answer:

- *Eclipse* is the third instalment of a franchise.
- We are given the plot summaries for both films.
- *Eclipse*'s target audience is 'mostly women and 15–24 year olds'.

In addition to that we know that both products are trailers, which gives us some idea of what to expect in terms of narrative, enigmas and target audiences.

> Question 2 Why are media products that *represent outsiders*, such as vampire films, so popular?

Figure 11
Exemplar paper from June 2012.

Section A

Answer **all** questions in Section A.

Read the information and the three questions below.

You will be shown two media products **three** times. In between these viewings you should make notes in response to the questions below. These notes will not be marked.

You should spend approximately 45 minutes answering the question in Section A.

Media Product One – The film trailer for *Eclipse* from www.eclipsethe movie.com

Eclipse is the third instalment of the Twilight Saga film franchise, released in the UK in July 2010. The official website says 'Bella once again finds herself surrounded by danger as Seattle is ravaged by a string of mysterious killings and a malicious vampire continues her quest for revenge. In the midst of it all, she is forced to choose between her love for Edward and her friendship with Jacob.' Edward is a vampire and Jacob is a werewolf.

The film is a mix of horror, romance and fantasy, with a UK cinema demographic of mostly women and 15–24 year olds. Although the film was a financial success, some reviews criticised the film.

The official website contains the trailer, downloadable photos, and online store and community links to Facebook, YouTube and Twitter.

Media Product Two – The film trailer for *Let the Right One In* from www.lettherightoneinmovie.com

Let the Right One In is a Swedish film released in the UK in August 2008. The official website describes the film as 'disturbing, darkly atmospheric, yet unexpectedly tender'. Oskar, a lonely 12 year old boy who is bullied at school, finds friendship and love with a young girl called Eli who turns out to be a vampire. Eli's arrival coincides with a series of gruesome attacks and deaths.

The film is a mix of horror, romance and drama. It was a critical success and won many awards at international film festivals. A US remake, *Let Me In*, was released in October 2010.

The official website contains the trailer, press reviews, photos and a link to buy the DVD.

Question 1

  Evaluate how the two trailers use the narrative technique of enigma to encourage the target audience to watch the films.   *(8 marks)*

Question 2

  Why are media products that represent outsiders, such as vampire films, so popular?

You may also refer to other media products to support your answer.
                                                            (12 marks)

Question 3

  Do you think that official and unofficial websites contribute to a film's box office success?

You should refer to other media products to support your answer.
                                                            (12 marks)

Again, consider the information you are given:

- The generic nature of the films (*Eclipse* is 'a mix of horror, romance and fantasy' whilst *Let The Right One In* is 'a mix of horror, romance and drama').
- The target audience for both films (noting that *Let The Right One In* 'was a critical success' winning 'awards at international film festivals' resulting in a US remake).

Question 3 Do you think that official and unofficial *websites* contribute to a film's *box office success*?

The information given on the paper explains what the website contains for both products, in addition to other information as already highlighted regarding the factors affecting the success of both films, such as target audience, genre and critical reception.

Exam tip

Read the paper carefully, underlining and highlighting keywords in the questions and information given about the media products.

How to answer the questions

Question 1

Question 1 will always require you to focus on the products themselves, asking you to show your knowledge of fundamental *media concepts* in applying them to the products. The exemplar question directs you to look at the use of enigma in the trailers, and past questions have required a focus on representation. Any of the media concepts could be the focus for this question, but remember it is different from MEST1, as you are only expected to focus on one media concept and not to complete a media language analysis. This question is worth *8 marks* as compared to the 12 for each of the other two questions. This means that ideally you should aim to spend approximately *12 minutes* writing your answer to the question. In order to gain a good mark you will need to *refer closely to the products*, and so you will need to focus fully during the screenings (assuming they are moving image/audio products), so that you can take some useful notes.

MARK SCHEME

So what is the examiner looking for? Here is an adapted version of the AQA mark scheme for question 1, for the top level:

Level 4 (7–8 marks)

A sophisticated analysis and evaluation, showing very good critical autonomy.

Sophisticated understanding of media concepts.

Supported by detailed references to both media products.

Articulate and engaged.

You can attain this level as long as you have prepared appropriately. Even though the exam hinges on unseen products, your preparation is key to success. In particular:

- Practise notetaking in response to products.
- Revise media concepts.
- Develop your exam technique by doing practice answers.
- Take note of your teacher's advice on improving your technique.
- Develop a system for tackling the question, making good use of the note-making time.

NOTE-MAKING FOR MOVING IMAGE PRODUCTS

If the product is in the form of a DVD, you will know in advance, as your teachers will be informed so that they can make arrangements for screening. The screening will proceed in very much the same way as outlined in the section for MEST1 on p. 36, although you will have two products instead of the one for MEST1. This means that you should check that you have paid equal attention to both products during note-making time.

You will be shown the products three times, and given a short time to take notes in between each showing.

- Use the first screening to make sure you understand the content and purpose of each product.
- After the *first screening* read question 1 again and make notes on the relevant concept:

  - Remember to focus on question 1 – don't just describe the products.
  - Leave plenty of space to add further notes.

- Focus fully on the concept (e.g. use of enigma) during the *second screening*:

  - Aim to develop your initial ideas.
  - Make notes on both products.
  - Make sure you note specific details from the products which you can use to support your points as you are rewarded for close reference to the products.
  - Check that your notes are complete enough to tackle the question – what do you need to focus on during the third and final viewing? Have you covered both products equally? Have you focused on the question? Do you need to add any more detail for the examples you are going to use?
  - Start to plan your answer, perhaps numbering points and organising your notes.

- Use the *third screening* to add any final details that you missed earlier on, thinking about how you are going to answer the question.

Everybody has their own preferred style of note-making, which may (or may not!) work for them. It is a good idea to think about how you are going to organise your notes beforehand, as they are going to form the plan for your first answer. This is where practice is really important. You need to feel confident and happy with the whole process of note-making.

> **NOTE**
>
> Your notes are not assessed by the examiner, so do not worry about presentation for their sake. Make use of the space in the answer book, but make sure you draw a line through your notes to show the examiner that they are not to be marked.

Your notes need to essentially cover two angles: examples from the products and analysis of the intended purpose and effect. You are rewarded for your analysis of the products – not just describing them.

A straightforward way to organise your notes could be into bullet points, but you may find it more effective to perhaps divide the page into two columns – one for each product. This will help organise your ideas and think about the differences and similarities between the two media products. Some students prefer to use mind mapping, and have two separate mind maps for the two products. You need to find out which method works best for you, by practising note-making in response to unseen products.

Activity

Watch the trailers for *Eclipse* and *Let The Right One In* (available on the internet) three times. Give yourself a couple of minutes in between each viewing to make notes following the advice given above. Make sure that you are focused on question 1.

Revision tip

Practise making notes on a range of different media products: adverts, film and games trailers, music videos, TV opening sequences, etc. Use the key concepts as a focus for your notes, and then think about the MEST3 topics and wider debates and theories you could use to analyse the products. Consider how the products compare to the ones you have prepared for your case studies. This will really help you in preparing for the unseen products, as you will become accustomed to responding purposefully to different media products.

NOTE-MAKING FOR PRINT PRODUCTS

You will need to adjust your approach to note-making if you are given print products, as clearly you will have the texts in front of you throughout the exam and will not have to rely on your notes made during the viewing time. Students prefer to have print products because they can look back at them at any point, and do not have to rely on their notes and memories. Nevertheless this can work against you, as sometimes the temptation is to describe the products in too much detail without focusing on the question.

Your strategy for note-making and planning your answer should follow the general outline for moving image products:

1   Familiarise yourself with the background information and question first – highlight key words; what is the concept you need to focus on for question 1?
2   Read through the texts and highlight/underline any examples which are relevant; make notes in the margin and around the text of anything that occurs to you when reading through.
3   Reread the question and then go through the texts again; make notes in bullet point form of the key points you will make about both texts in answer to question 1. You need to bear in mind:

a. The point you want to make
b. The evidence in the product to support it.

4   Organise your notes by numbering them in order to plan your answer. Decide which is the main point for each of the products as this could be your starting point for your answer.
5   If you have any time left over, think about question 2 and the examples you could use from each product as regards the focus of the question.

Activity

Practise making notes about a range of different print and e-media products – try exploring products which you are not familiar with, such as products with different target audiences in mind. Focus your notes on specific media concepts, for example:

*   narrative
*   genre conventions
*   media language.

SHAPING YOUR ANSWER

critical analysis
The process of questioning a media product, considering it within the larger context of how it is typical of the media industry as a whole, and what it suggests regarding the audience and society. Critical analysis is about selecting relevant theories and perspectives to investigate the media product.

Your notes will form the basis for your answer for question 1. You need to write in a formal essay style, rather than as notes (see section on essay writing in MEST1 Section B (p. 75) for more advice on this). You need to be analytical in your approach, focusing on the question, but extending your comments by discussing purpose, issues and effects. Your focus should be on *critical analysis*.

To illustrate what this means, let us consider our exemplar question from June 2012. The question asks you to 'evaluate' the use of narrative enigmas. Possible points could include:

evaluate
To assess importance or usefulness; explore the strengths and weaknesses of a particular approach, technique or device; explore the effectiveness of something.

*   How both trailers use enigmas to intrigue and involve the target audience as part of a marketing campaign; discussing the reasoning behind this approach.
*   A discussion of how *Eclipse* is typical of Hollywood in terms of making the plot more explicit, targeting a mass audience, whereas *Let The Right One In* is more mysterious with extensive use of enigmas, targeting an art-house audience who enjoy more challenging and offbeat narratives.

- How both trailers use enigmas to market the films by creating mystery and excitement.
- Discuss the contrasting use of enigma in both films regarding relationships and romance, considering the context of Hollywood and European cinema.
- Explore how enigmas are used to appeal to different target audiences – for example, focus on stars, violence, special effects and horror.
- Explore how the *Eclipse* trailer relies on audience pre-knowledge, being part of the Twilight franchise and therefore relies less on enigma than on special effects and stars.
- Explore how *Let The Right One In* uses enigma to emphasise the vampire horror genre conventions to appeal to a wider audience.

Question 1 checklist

- Read questions and information carefully.
- Stay focused on question 1 when making notes during screenings of products.
- Organise notes effectively to plan your answer.
- Make detailed reference to both products in your answer.
- Don't repeat yourself – try to include a range of points.
- Only spend around 12 minutes on this question.
- Make sure you stay focused on the question and the relevant media concept.
- Analyse and evaluate – don't merely describe.

Questions 2 and 3

These two questions require a slightly different approach from the first question. You are required to draw on your study of the media over the whole of your course, your wider knowledge and your case studies. You will need to demonstrate your knowledge of *relevant debates*, *theories* and *wider contexts*, making reference to other relevant products to develop your answers.

These two questions are worth more marks than question 1, and therefore will require you to spend more time answering them. Each question is worth 12 marks, and therefore you should aim to spend approximately 15 minutes on each. You need to write in a formal essay style.

In order to gain a higher-level mark, you will need to be able to develop a more sophisticated and sustained discussion of the issues, developing your own standpoint, which you can explain and justify. An important skill is to be able to recognise other standpoints, and develop a *debate* between different positions. For example, it may be relevant to discuss a feminist or Marxist viewpoint regarding particular media products in contrast to the dominant ideological position.

The examiner is looking for your ability to *evaluate* and develop a *critical analysis* of the products in the light of relevant debates, issues and wider contexts. Nevertheless this is not merely about listing theories, but also about being able to apply relevant theories to the products to develop a range of points in answer to the question.

Your answer should aim to:

- focus precisely on the question
- have a clear argument
- engage with relevant debates, explaining the significance of specific aspects of the products
- support your points with evidence from the products and other examples
- evaluate different perspectives, arguments and approaches
- refer to relevant theories, and explain their significance to the question and products
- avoid repetition, irrelevance and generalisation.

Exam tip

You have been told before, and doubtlessly will be told again: *spend time planning your answer before writing!* Spend a couple of minutes noting down some key issues/debates and examples of products before launching into your answer. Try to organise your notes before writing.

Let's take a look at how this works in practice, using the past paper questions on *Eclipse* and *Let The Right One In*.

Question 2: Why are media products that represent outsiders, such as vampire films, so popular? You may also refer to other media products to support your answer.

We have already established that this is a question that is essentially about representation, but your answer needs to situate the representations within the wider contexts, debates and theories surrounding the products. Question 2 will always offer you the option to 'refer to other media products', whereas question 3 will state that you '*should* refer to other products'.

The AQA mark scheme for the top level is looking for the following:

Level 4 (10–12 marks)

A sophisticated evaluation, showing very good critical autonomy.

Detailed and sophisticated application of a wide range of media debates, issues and theories.

Supports answer with a wide range of examples from other media.

Articulate and engaged.

You can attain this level by:

- revising case studies, noting key debates, issues and theories
- listing media products covered throughout your study of the media, and noting relevant points regarding contexts and debates
- using past papers online to get further exam practice
- acting on your teacher's feedback to practice questions.

To answer question 2 take the following approach:

- Discuss the 'unseen' media products in the light of the question topic – for example, representation of outsiders.
- Apply relevant theories, debates and issues.
- Make reference to other media products which are comparable.

With our exemplar question this means that you need to consider what the products' representation of outsiders shows in terms of the film industry and the broader media context as a whole. This could result in the following points:

- Genre conventions of the vampire horror – relating this to genre theory, and giving examples of the genre, in film and television (e.g. *True Blood, Dracula*).
- Audience appeal in terms of nature of target audiences and pleasures offered by the genre, considering relevant theory such as uses and gratifications or Dyer's utopian pleasures.
- The nature of the target audiences in terms of demographics and psychographics, considering how mainstream media such as Hollywood constructs representations to engage with their audience. This could be extended to consider representations of outsiders in other media such as the music industry and computer games.
- Narrative theory in terms of how classic Hollywood narrative revolves around conflict and is character driven; you could refer to Levi-Strauss and binary oppositions.

- Audience positioning: encouraging audience to relate to the underdog/outsider, taking sides to be involved in the narrative.

   Question 3 Do you think that official and unofficial websites contribute to a film's box office success? You should refer to other media products to support your answer.

The AQA mark scheme for the top level for this question is looking for an answer that is:

Level 4 (10–12 marks)

A sophisticated and detailed evaluation, showing very good critical autonomy.

Sophisticated and detailed application of a wide range of wider contexts.

Supports answer with a wide range of examples from other media.

Articulate and engaged.

Your approach should be very similar to that for question 2, except you *must* refer to other media products. The mark scheme is asking for a 'wide range' of examples to support your points. The balance should be less on the 'unseen' products and more on your own examples. Your starting point will be the unseen products before going on to debate the issues, structuring an evaluation of the relevant contexts and showing your understanding of relevant arguments. Notice that the mark scheme is asking you to apply a 'wide range of wider contexts', so that you are considering the topic from a range of perspectives, drawing on your studies. Your approach should aim to:

- introduce the topic by explaining relevance to the unseen products
- debate how the products are typical of the media industry as a whole in this respect
- extend discussion to compare products to other examples, examining the wider issues and debates regarding the media industry
- conclude by evaluating how the 'unseen' products are typical of the industry as a whole
- consider what this demonstrates about the media as a whole.

With specific reference to our exemplar questions your answer could include some of the following points:

- The effectiveness of websites as a marketing tool: typical content and techniques used to interest the target audience.

- How effective are websites in reaching different target audiences – are they more suitable for specific demographics?
- What other marketing tools are used by the film industry – for example, trailers, poster campaigns, stars, using other media?
- Hollywood's reliance on a range of other strategies to attract audiences – for example, remakes, adaptations of successful book series, TV series and computer games, stars, new technology (3D).
- Appeal of websites in terms of the interactive audience.
- The advantages of new technology in fostering audience involvement and developing fan following – for example using social networking sites such as Facebook.
- Issues regarding the film industry and merchandising, using new technology to sell DVDs and further associated merchandise.

Your aim should be to draw on your knowledge of film websites, the film industry and wider media trends to evaluate examples of other media products in discussing your points.

Questions 2 and 3 checklist

- Use the 'unseen' products to initiate wider discussion of media issues and debates.
- Make use of relevant theory to develop discussion of the products and issues.
- Stay focused on the question.
- Structure a debate of the relevant topic.
- Question 3 must focus on your own examples.
- Make sure you don't repeat yourself.
- Analyse, evaluate and debate.
- Use up-to-date and relevant examples of other media products.
- Try to extend your discussion to consider a number of different arguments and perspectives.
- Make sure that you do not repeat points you have made in answer to another question.

Exemplar answers

Media Studies is different from many of your other subjects in that your answer is not being marked on account of it being 'right' or 'wrong'. The examiner is not looking for a particular answer but is looking to reward you for your level of understanding and knowledge, and how you have applied this to the unseen products. All students will be coming from a different background in terms of their choice of case studies and other media products that they have studied in the two years. There are no set products for Media Studies, just the two case study topics which all students have in common. Likewise you may well have studied a range of contextual topics and theories different from those studied by other students. Nevertheless there is still a lot of common ground for the study of the media, particularly in terms of needing to be familiar with all the media concepts, and certain key debates and issues, such as the impact of new technology on the media. What this means is that there is no one set answer which is 'perfect'. It is a question of you having a confident knowledge of the products, issues, theories, debates and case studies that you have studied, and being able to apply them to the unseen products.

The following exemplar answers are therefore not exhaustive in terms of covering everything, or indeed being perfect. They are for you to use as an example of how to actually write the answers to the questions, particularly thinking about the style required by the answers. These answers are in response to the MEST3 Section A questions from June 2011.

Media Product One – Adidas House Party Advert

Adidas launched the House Party campaign in January 2009. The advert was part of the Adidas Originals brand campaign which used television, cinema, print and online platforms. The Adidas website described the campaign as 'set against the backdrop of a house party hosting an electric mix of people from the worlds of music, fashion and sport'. The advert includes David Beckham, the Ting Tings, Estelle, Missy Elliot, Katy Perry, Method Man and Run DMC. The song in the advert is the Pilooski remix of Frankie Valli's original version of 'Beggin''. Adidas also created a version of the advert which enabled users to click on various points of the film to view extra footage. XBox Live also hosted a dedicated Adidas Originals section on its portal where gamers could browse and download content.

Media Product Two – NHS and Home Office Advert

The £4m campaign targeted 18 to 24 year olds with the slogan, 'You wouldn't start a night like this, so why end it that way?' There were two TV adverts in the campaign, one focusing on a young man and one on a young woman getting ready to go out. The campaign used TV, radio, press and digital platforms. The TV adverts appeared on youth programming, sport and music channels; the radio adverts on national and regional stations; and the print adverts in youth-oriented titles including *Nuts*, *NME*, *Glamour* and *Reveal*. In the *Guardian*, Jacqui Smith, the Home Secretary at the time, said: 'This new campaign will challenge people to think twice about the serious consequences of losing control. Binge drinking is not only damaging to health but it makes individuals vulnerable to harm.'

Question 1 Evaluate how each media product represents young people.

(8 marks)

Question 2 Why are shock tactics, such as those in media product two, so often used? You may also refer to other media products to support your answer.

(12 marks)

Question 3 Consider the value of using online marketing to target a youth audience. You should refer to other media products to support your answer.

(12 marks)

Question 1: Evaluate how each media product represents young people.

The first media product, an advertisement for Adidas, features a sequence of shots of various celebrities who would be instantly recognisable to young people. The implication is that young people value celebrity, and would want to emulate their idols in terms of their party lifestyle and ultimately their association with the Adidas brand. The Adidas advert represents young people as hedonistic by representing the brand as associated with fun and socialising, clearly a lifestyle towards which the target audience would aspire.

The second product, the Drink Aware adverts, also represent young people as hedonistic, yet this is represented in a negative light as being destructive and anti-social. A montage is used to show the two young people getting ready to go out, but shocks the audience with disturbing imagery such as ripping clothing, urinating on the floor and smearing a take-away over their clothes. Ultimately the message is that young people are out of control and self-destructive, a negative stereotype which can be found across the media as part of a larger moral panic about the behaviour and attitudes of youth.

The contrasting representations in the two campaigns are constructed through the use of lighting and *mise en scène*. Both of the binge drinking adverts were set in ordinary domestic settings that the target audience could relate to, using a frenetic contemporary music soundtrack to create a party atmosphere in contrast to the progressively disturbing imagery. Likewise the Adidas advert uses the Pilooski soundtrack to create a feeling of excitement and energy which complements the imagery in creating a party atmosphere, contrasting fast-paced editing with slow-motion action, featuring shots of dancing, seduction and gambling. Adidas represents partying as aspirational for young people wanting to emulate the lifestyles of their heroes – both male and female – whereas the Drink Aware adverts represent young people's lifestyles as shocking and disturbing, where the pursuit of pleasure leads to self-destruction.

Question 2: Why are shock tactics, such as those in media product two, so often used? You may also refer to other media products to support your answer.

It could be argued that shock tactics are overused in advertising, particularly in public information and charity adverts. The Drink Aware adverts are typical in this respect, seeking to grab the target audience's attention through the use of disturbing images such as the vomiting and urination used to represent the harrowing consequences of drinking too much. The adverts create enigmas, as the audience are increasingly disturbed by the images, hooked to discover what the advert could possibly be promoting, and therefore more effectively getting its message across.

Shock tactics have been used extensively to grab the audience's attention – for example, in campaigns run by the NSPCC and for road safety. In these adverts the shock is heightened by using imagery of vulnerable children and young people, which prove particularly emotive and therefore effective in getting the message across. Advertisers clearly consider audience psychographics in using imagery which will prompt viewers to change their behaviour, take action and give money in the case of charities. The realism of these adverts heightens the shock, using actors, locations and situations which audiences can relate to, in appearing to be everyday and ordinary.

One of the dangers of using shock tactics is that they can be overused, and audiences may become desensitised and ultimately resistant to the intended messages of the adverts. It could be argued that the media is saturated with shocking imagery, in terms of films, news footage and computer games in particular, and therefore shock tactics are less effective, and the target audience may be quite cynical when confronted with such imagery. However, the message of the Drink Aware adverts is undermined by the message of other media products, such as the Adidas campaign and programmes such as *Skins*, which present the hedonistic lifestyle as fun and attractive. David Morley argued that audiences don't always accept the preferred meaning, and in this respect the shock tactics encoded in the advert may not have been decoded as the producers intended, as the target audience is situated in a very different culture from the advertisers.

Question 3: Consider the value of using online marketing to target a youth audience. You should refer to other media products to support your answer.

Online marketing has become one of the main platforms for reaching youth audiences in recent years, as their use of traditional media platforms has declined whilst the internet has become more popular with this demographic. Advertisers have struggled to reach the youth audience in the past, but the internet offers the advantage of being able to target individuals more effectively, as sites such as Amazon and Ebay track users' profiles and target them with specific products. The huge success of social networking sites with a youth demographic has made them a particularly effective way of targeting users for advertisers.

Lady Gaga has led the way in terms of marketing techniques, as she has made use of Twitter and Facebook to cultivate her fanbase of 'little monsters', being an effective way of reaching a global audience. The advantage of such online marketing techniques is that it encourages audience interactivity, making them feel part of a community and cultivating their loyalty to the 'brand'. By 'liking' Lady Gaga on Facebook you are effectively marketing the brand to your friends, making you an opinion leader as in the two-step flow response theory. Nevertheless, Lady Gaga continues to use more traditional marketing techniques alongside new media, for example deliberately creating controversy in order to attract media interest as with the advert for her new fragrance in which she is depicted naked, except for miniature figures of men crawling over her.

One of the advantages of online marketing is that convergence has enabled the technology to reach audiences at any time, and in any place, facilitated by the widespread use of smartphones, games consoles and laptops in particular. Brands such as Red Bull have been quick to build on the opportunities offered to reach a youth audience, through the use of a viral marketing campaign which harnesses the potential of social networking and the global nature of the internet. Brands such as Childline have tried to develop brand awareness by launching an interactive campaign 'How U Feelin?' which asked users to remix the advert online to enter a competition. This helped to create a positive and modern image for the charity, as well as getting its message across as being relevant to the lives of young people.

Activity

Read through the answers above and have a go at writing your own version, using your own examples and theories prepared for your case studies.

Working through an exemplar paper (2)

The following exemplar is in the style of the AQA exam. Have a look at the websites and the questions, and then plan your own answers before looking at the ideas listed below.

**www.bbc.co.uk/radio1/
surgery/**

Media Product One – the website homepage for *The Surgery* with Aled from BBC Radio One

The Surgery is a weekly radio show broadcast on Sunday evenings between 9pm and 10pm. It is also available on the BBC i-player for a week after initial broadcast. The programme aims to provide its audience with advice and help on a range of subjects including sexuality, depression and exam stress. The presenter, Aled Haydn Jones, takes calls from listeners alongside a regular panel of doctors and experts. The website features advice pages, helpful links and factfiles on popular topics.

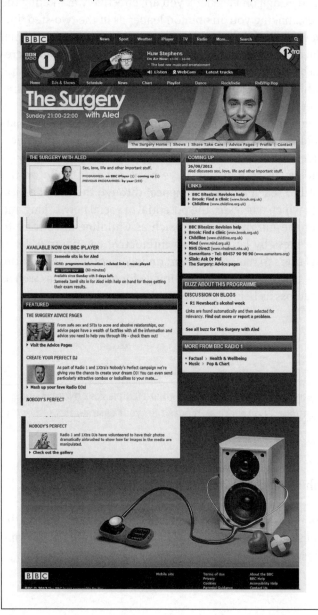

Figure 12
Homepage for BBC Radio 1's
The Surgery.

Media Product Two – the website homepage for Classic FM

Classic FM is a national commercial radio station which is devoted to broadcasting popular classical music. The station is owned by Global Radio, which is Britain's largest commercial radio organisation and is responsible for other stations such as Xfm and Heart. The website for Classic FM displays the schedule alongside features on composers, presenters, news stories regarding classical music, competitions and reviews of new releases.

Question 1 Evaluate how the two media products represent their audiences.

(8 marks)

Question 2 What is the appeal to audiences of such websites? You may refer to other media products to support your answer.

(12 marks)

Question 3 Do you think that the interactive potential of new media technology contributes to the success of some media products? You should refer to other media products to support your answer.

(12 marks)

Figure 13

Homepage for Classic FM.

The following points are meant to be guidance for what you could include in answer to the questions. It is certainly not meant to be a definitive plan for an answer, just an indication of a possible approach. You will find that perhaps you may not have covered a particular debate or theory, or that you will have other points which would be equally valid.

QUESTION 1: EVALUATE HOW THE TWO MEDIA PRODUCTS CONSTRUCT THEIR AUDIENCES.

> **NOTE**
>
> Question 1 will always require you to analyse one aspect of the media concepts in relation to the two unseen products, requiring you to make detailed reference to both products.
>
> This question is essentially about audience, and how audience is represented in each of the products. What do the two products tell us about the target audiences? What do we learn about in terms of demographic and psychographic profile of the target audience? Are there any similarities and differences in terms of target audience and the two products? Do the products construct a cultural and social identity in terms of their target audience?

The website for BBC Radio 1's *The Surgery* has a very clear sense of its target audience, particularly in terms of age group and values, attitudes and lifestyle.

- Bright primary colours create a very positive and upbeat tone for the page; Aled is smiling directly at the audience, contributing to a welcoming and youthful mode of address. This is maintained in the register of the language used on the page, which creates a sense of community for a youth audience. Simple imagery creates an appropriate message regarding the aim of the website, with two hearts symbolising love and relationships – one of the hearts has a plaster on it, suggesting an injury which has been healed – presumably with the help of *The Surgery*. This mildly humorous image is matched by the stethoscope which is listening to a mobile phone, again using simple imagery to communicate the purpose of the site and the radio programme.
- In terms of institution it is very clear that the website targets a youth audience, thus satisfying the BBC's public service broadcasting remit. The ideals put in place by the first Director General of the BBC, Sir John Reith, argued that the BBC should inform, educate and entertain ALL sectors of society. In this respect the website maintains the brand image

of the BBC, and Radio 1 in particular, with images of familiar DJs, links to Radio 1's live broadcasting and the familiar BBC logo.

- The youth audience is represented as being interested in celebrity, in particular as regards sport and music, with reference to stars who would be instantly recognisable to the target audience, such as David Ginola and Olly Murs. All the features on the page use familiar faces in terms of celebrities and radio personalities to help engage the audience. The star image of these celebrities is utilised to appeal to the audience.

- The range of features suggests that the youth audience faces problems and stresses. The title 'The Surgery' suggests this is a place the troubled audience can turn to for help. In this respect the programme satisfies the BBC's remit to inform, in contrast to the majority of the rest of the output of Radio 1, which is concerned with entertainment. The problems featured suggest a teen audience, with a focus on exam stress and revision techniques.

- The youth audience is targeted with the links to social networking sites such as Facebook and the clear accessible layout of the page.

In contrast you may be less confident writing about the Classic FM website, as it may well be unfamiliar to you. Nevertheless, this is a central point to this product, as its target audience has a very different cultural and social identity.

- In terms of identity, the page makes assumptions regarding age group and social class. The style of the page is much more cluttered and formal in terms of mode of address, using a serif font for headings and subdued colour palate for the page as a whole. The page assumes common interests and frameworks of knowledge amongst its audience, with references to classical musicians and composers, implying a well-educated target audience, or perhaps an audience which aspires to be better educated regarding culture, with features such as 'A beginner's guide to Mozart's operas'. The mode of address and cultural references imply a target audience aged 40 years and upwards. The page clearly tries to appeal to an older audience who have some disposable income, with adverts for cruises and holidays which offer 'total luxury'. This suggests that a sizeable proportion of the audience are retired, middle class and reasonably well off with a desire to learn about 'highbrow' culture.

- Nevertheless the page suggests that its target audience are more aspirational in terms of their cultural identity, as it offers opportunities to add to their knowledge with the 'Beginner's Guide'. It also suggests an audience who wish to improve themselves in other ways, as with the feature

'Classical music for working out', which also confirms an ageing audience who are keen to maintain fitness.

- The site constructs a sense of community which encompasses the listeners, presenters and musicians. The mode of address is friendly and informal overall, addressing the audience directly, and using a humorous tone in places. This sense of community is further developed by the Facebook feature which displays some of the listeners who 'like' Classic FM. This offers the possible gratification of personal relationships in line with Blumler and Katz's uses and gratifications theory, along with other uses such as providing information and entertainment.

- The website also suggests an older audience who are happy with new media technologies, with the references to Facebook, the link to Twitter, and the reference to digital technologies such as the Kindle and iPhone. This goes against the predominant stereotype of ageing audiences being averse to modern technology, representing them as embracing new technology.

QUESTION 2: WHAT IS THE APPEAL TO AUDIENCES OF SUCH WEBSITES? YOU MAY REFER TO OTHER MEDIA PRODUCTS TO SUPPORT YOUR ANSWER.

NOTE

Remember that with question 2 most of your answer will still focus on the two media products, but this question is about media issues and debates, so you need to go further and think about how the products are typical of radio institutions and the broadcasting industry as a whole. Do they show any trends which are typical of the contemporary media industry?

Think about the uses and gratifications such websites can provide for audiences. How is the audience positioned regarding the broadcaster? How does the website try to market the actual radio station? Does it try to promote other products? Are there any theories which you can refer to when making your points? Remember to use plenty of examples from the websites, as well as from other products to support your points.

- Both websites offer a sense of community to their target audiences, but for different uses. In terms of Blumler and Katz's theory, *The Surgery* website offers information and education, but critically appeals to the need for personal identity, offering 'all the information and advice you need to help you through life'. Its features allow the audience to relate to the situations they read about, and offer reassurance and advice. The audience can compare themselves to the case studies, which can be gratifying in terms of making them feel better about their own situation, or perhaps suggesting that they are not alone.

- Dyer's theory of utopian pleasures can be applied to both websites to demonstrate how they offer escape from the fragmented, harsh realities of real life for their target audience. *The Surgery* offers transparency in its openness about intimate matters, offering information which the audience may find difficult to access in the outside world, and both sites offer a sense of community and intimacy through their use of direct address and access to the stars. Music stars' websites and use of Twitter are examples of other ways in which audiences can use digital technology to gain access to a wider, yet seemingly intimate community, as with Lady Gaga's 'little monsters'.

- Websites can be very important for radio stations as they offer a different platform for accessing the products. They construct a visual image for the station, which before digital technology relied on sound to create a brand image. Both sites feature links to live broadcasting as well as picturing presenters. Classic FM goes further in advertising other shows, a range of features and also adverts for associated products. In the broader music industry the introduction of digital technology has enabled products to extend their brand image and audience by using different platforms; the music magazine *Kerrang!* launched a digital radio station as well as a television channel.

- The websites are typical of what David Gauntlett refers to as 'pick and mix' media, allowing the audience the opportunity to select what features and links they wish to consume, in contrast to consumption of traditional media forms, where there is little choice. The Classic FM website uses a layout which is similar to a scrapbook, allowing the audience to decide what they want to do. This is a fundamental appeal of the internet, where websites such as the *Kerrang!* website allow the audience extensive choice – whether to find out news, watch videos, listen to the radio or read reviews.

- A major appeal of such websites is that they are easily accessible, with new technology making the internet portable and available just about everywhere. The layout of the websites makes them even more readily accessible and easy to use.

QUESTION 3: DO YOU THINK THAT THE INTERACTIVE POTENTIAL OF NEW MEDIA TECHNOLOGY CONTRIBUTES TO THE SUCCESS OF SOME MEDIA PRODUCTS? YOU SHOULD REFER TO OTHER MEDIA PRODUCTS TO SUPPORT YOUR ANSWER.

> **NOTE**
>
> The starting point for question 3 remains the two unseen products, yet the majority of your answer should be based around your own examples. You should use your own examples to develop discussion of the wider context which is core to question 3. There will be relevant information within the introduction to both products which you can use in your answer. You should aim to make different points to your answer to question 2, even though there might be some overlap between the two questions.
>
> What is the appeal of interactivity to audiences? How is it used on the internet? How is it used on other platforms? Does it have any advantages for media institutions? What impact has interactivity had on the way in which audiences consume the media?
>
> You can use specific examples from the two unseen products before going on to discuss other media products.

- Interactivity gives the audience a sense of ownership in terms of their relationship with media products; audiences can select what they want to consume, and when (e.g. Classic FM lists the different options for listening to the station; the BBC uses the iPlayer as a way of providing access to past broadcasts; Channel 4 have C4OD).
- Links to social networking sites mean that audiences can develop a closer relationship with media products, keeping up to date with the latest news, and being able to participate in online forums. This helps satisfy the need for social interaction as identified by Blumler and Katz.
- Audiences can become producers as interactivity allows them to contribute and share their own content; YouTube is an example of a website which is centred on user-generated content.
- More traditional media have tried to develop their brand image by cultivating greater interactivity, especially by using other platforms. Convergence has led to changes in how audiences consume media products, enabling them to be more selective and use different platforms. The generic term 'Web 2.0' was coined to describe the concept of the internet as a dynamic platform where users are accustomed to having a dynamic relationship with the media, participating and sharing, as well as consuming. A range of contemporary media products could be cited to illustrate this, starting with radio websites and examples which you have studied.

- Media products have increasingly sought to promote interactivity, as it is a means of marketing the product as well as encouraging audience feedback without investing in expensive market research. Television shows such as *Big Brother* and *The Only Way Is Essex* are examples of transmedia products which have cultivated interactivity, harnessing a range of platforms in order to create more publicity and be more widely accessible for their target audiences.

Examiners' advice for MEST3 Section A

- Focus on the question and the area being assessed.
- Divide your time according to the marks available.
- Make a range of different points to get a good mark.
- Prepare for the exam by studying a wide range of media products, and think about how they link to the issues you have studied.
- Use your own examples to support and explain the points you are making.
- Try to use examples that are quite different from the exam products to demonstrate issues and debates; don't just use examples that are very similar.
- Try to use original and up-to-date examples.
- Make detailed reference to the media products.
- Question 1 does not require a media language analysis – focus on the concept in the question.
- Use theory to support points for questions 2 and 3.
- Try to develop a sense of debate in questions 2 and 3.
- Include your own opinion if you can support it with media debates, issues, theories and examples from other media products for questions 2 and 3.

Summary of revision strategies for MEST3 Section A

- Make a list of relevant theories and debates covered during your case studies.
- Revise the media concepts.
- Use the past papers on the AQA website to practise answers and to familiarise yourself with the style of questions.
- Go through any practice papers you have done and think about how you could improve them.
- Make a list of possible products you could refer to as examples for the two topic areas.
- Read through the exemplar candidate answers on the AQA website.
- Make a list of useful media terminology.

MEST3 CRITICAL PERSPECTIVES SECTION B

Assessment at a glance: Section B

- MEST3 Section B is based upon a case study you have completed.
- Two pre-set topic areas are available for investigation. For the June 2014 exam these are 'representations in the media' and 'the impact of new/digital media' but these are subject to change in future years.
- You will have chosen your own case study and completed it independently, with guidance from your teacher/tutor.
- It is assessed by an examination in which you will choose one essay question from a choice of two on each of the topics available.
- The essay is marked out of 48, making it worth 60% of the whole of MEST3.
- You have one hour to complete your answer.
- Two assessment objectives are tested.
- It is a synoptic unit.

MEST3 topics are subject to change. You can get up-to-date information either from your teacher or by visiting the AQA website.

The topics that you need to study for MEST3 are subject to change. You need to check with your teacher to make sure you are revising the appropriate topics. If you are taking the exam in June 2014, then the topics are 'representations in the media' and 'the impact of new/digital media'. For future exams from June 2015, one of the topics will again be 'the impact of new/digital media' but the second will be a study based upon 'audience and identity'. If there are any further changes to the topics offered in subsequent years, you can find this information by referring to the AQA website.

Updated guidance for topics is available on the A2 website: http://cw.routledge.com/textbooks/a2mediastudies/

Introduction to Section B

In the second part of the MEST3 examination, you will spend an hour producing one essay response to a question based upon the two topics offered by the awarding body: 'representations in the media' and 'the impact of new/digital media'. The essay is marked out of 48 and preparation is by the case studies which you have been working on in readiness for the examination. For each of these topics, two questions will be available and so you will need to choose one question from the four offered. This means that a crucial decision will need to be made. Although it may sound clichéd to say that this decision may affect the outcome of your overall grade, it is also palpably true. You will need to reject three of the questions and focus entirely on the question that remains. Your decision about which questions to reject is simplified by the fact that two of them relate to the topic you won't be responding to, but there will still be a choice between the other two questions which do relate to the topic you are going to answer, so there is still a decision to make. To make matters worse, this decision must be made fairly quickly, as the time for thinking, planning and constructing your response is all included in this one hour. You must be selective and take care when thinking about which question to tackle and your guiding principle should be to consider which of them best gives you the opportunity to demonstrate your knowledge, your abilities to analyse, evaluate and refer extensively to examples and relevant theories; in other words, you need to pick the question you feel you can score the best mark by doing.

Assessment objectives

As a second year A level student who is preparing for Section B of the MEST3 examination, you will doubtless be very familiar with the assessment objectives which are present in the course. Assessment objectives define what you are being tested on in a subject; they are the awarding body's way of letting both teachers and students know what they are looking for in a response to a unit, and more specifically in response to the tasks which have been set. For both sections of MEST3, there are two assessment objectives which need to be addressed.

- AO1: demonstrate knowledge and understanding of media concepts, contexts and critical debates.
- AO2: apply knowledge and understanding when analysing media products and processes (and evaluating own practical work) to show how meanings and responses are created.

These two assessment objectives are the same two as those you will have focused upon in the MEST1 examination you completed as part of the AS level assessment, but the emphasis within the AOs is slightly different this time around. In this MEST3 examination, which like the other units is worth 25% of the overall A-level qualification, 10% from the 25% comes from AO1 and 15% from AO2. This may seem a little confusing, but it is important to remember that in MEST3 there is more of a focus on AO2 than on AO1, whereas MEST1 had more emphasis on AO1 than on AO2. Even within the

MEST3 unit there is disparity as there is greater emphasis on AO2 in Section B than there is in Section A.

This is partly explained by the fact that now, in the position you find yourself in – an A2 level student – you are expected to be much more experienced in applying your knowledge and understanding (the focus of AO1) to the real media world and the processes which take place in media production and in the media industries (the focus of AO2). Concepts, contexts and debates are the basic tools of the subject and your knowledge and understanding of these have helped you to produce analyses of products, explain features using concepts of language, representation and audience, to understand conventions of narrative and genre and generally to make the progress required for a successful completion of the AS qualification. But AO2 forms a bigger part of the A2 than it did at AS because, at this level, you are expected to have more knowledge of the workings of media in the real world.

A closer look at the MEST3 Section B unit content

In your preparation for Section B of MEST3, you will have experienced both constraints in that you must prepare to answer a question on a pre-set topic and freedom in that you choose only one of those pre-set topics to answer. Within your preparation, and since the specification makes it clear that candidates should produce a case study of their own design covering an area they choose, there is plenty of flexibility for you in each of the topic areas.

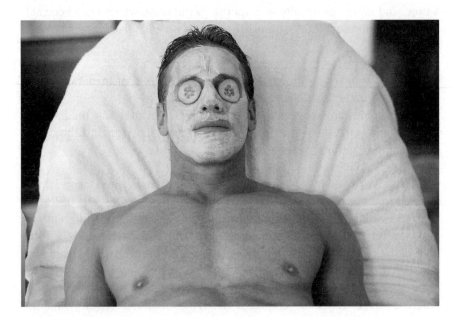

Figure 14

Man having facial, an example of a certain representation of masculinity which you might investigate for the topic of representation.

Let's take a look at what the awarding body suggest your case studies might investigate.

Areas you might investigate for representations:

- How particular groups or places are shown across a range of media
- Possible alternative representations, that is, those not usually commonly associated with the subject or those originating in non-mainstream media
- Representation and stereotyping
- Representation and genre
- Representations and wider contexts
- Representations and audience
- Cross-cultural factors in representation
- The effect of globalisation on representations in the media
- Values and ideology underlying representations.

Figure 15
Girl using laptop.

Areas you might investigate for new/digital media:

- The interactive consumer
- Social networking
- The internet and world wide web
- Blogs
- Podcasts
- The changing contemporary media landscape
- The role of media institutions
- The impact on democracy of new/digital media
- The changing role of the distributor and exhibitor
- New technologies and the audience
- Mobile technologies and the audience
- The effect of globalisation on the use of new/digital media
- Cross-cultural factors in the use and effects of new/digital media
- Values and ideology and the impact of new technology.

These are fairly thorough lists on each of the two topics offered, and the amount of knowledge and understanding you will need of each of these areas depends upon the nature of the case study you are undertaking. Some of these potential case study research areas (e.g. ideological aspects or the role of media institutions or new technologies and the audience) are universally relevant to any area of media your case study is based upon. Others (e.g. social networking) will require more depth if the case study looks at the expansion of Twitter or Facebook rather than, for example, the impact of new/digital technology on news, although that is not to say that social networking is irrelevant to that particular topic. What is required is for you to decide which of these topic areas are important in your preparation for your case study.

The specification is clear in that it requires you to undertake case studies from within the three media platforms of print, broadcast and digital Web-based media (e-media). Therefore, in keeping with the spirit of the subject at this level in which the intention is to give you a broad experience of the media, you cannot focus upon an area which appeals to you the most; rather you need to approach your case studies with more of a cross-media approach. The specification makes several suggestions about what specifically you might investigate in preparing your case studies. Among these suggestions are: for the representations topic, a look at newspaper representations of refugees in Britain, Los Angeles as represented in American film, or teenagers in soap operas and British films; for the new media topic, an investigation of YouTube or Wikipedia in connection with mobile technology or MySpace in connection with social networking.

Remember that these are suggestions made by the awarding body and that there is nothing to stop you from exploring your own choice of topic from within the relevant area of media. After all, media is an evolving and changing entity and no doubt a new representation or e-media or digital technology will have emerged in the interim between the publication of the specification and your examination. You might consider, for example, the impact of the Leveson Report into press standards on new technology in the way newspapers are consumed, or the redefining of the representations of the Middle East and North Africa following the Arab Spring uprisings and their aftermath.

It is worth reiterating here that the case study needs to be product-based with an array of examples of actual media products which, depending upon the exact focus of the case study, should cover many different angles such as media products from different periods of time, different countries and various cultures and across the different media forms of print, broadcasting and digital Web-based media.

Guidance is further offered in the specification on how a theoretical approach could be adopted in your case studies to address a number of issues and debates as shown in the following box.

Case studies could involve a theoretical approach to cover a number of issues and debates.

Representations in the media

- The construction of representations of groups and places
- Issues surrounding political representations
- The effects of representations on audiences and the reasons why representations exist as they do
- Consider cross-cultural factors in the representation of groups and places.

New/digital media

- The impact of new/digital technology on construction of media products
- Political and social implications of new technology and the methods of their consumption
- The historical, current and future effects on media institutions
- The role of the interactive audience
- Cross-cultural factors and the effects of globalisation.

So, crucially for Section B, good quality preparation and planning are required. A thorough knowledge of the case study you have undertaken is, needless to say, essential. You will have read, watched, downloaded, listened to and looked up a wide variety of material which offers a variety of opinions, examples and theories. This next section will look more closely at the different types of research you will have done and how you will use that research to respond to questions in the exam.

Synopticity

It is common for A2 examinations across a range of disciplines to award a synoptic mark in the final examination of a subject which, for Media Studies, is MEST3. MEST4 is a coursework unit and one which you may well complete prior to the MEST3 examination. Synopticity poses a further set of challenges to candidates in addition to those already inherent in an advanced course of study.

Broadly speaking, synopticity in media is achieved in three ways and Section B of the MEST3 facilitates these very well. To show synoptic ability, you must be able to:

1. Draw upon your experiences in studying media both in analysing media products and in your own production and show a link between the knowledge and understanding you have gained across the whole experience you have had of the subject.
2. Refer extensively and with confidence to the key concepts of the subject which act like the subject's building blocks.
3. Apply critical wider debates and issues in responses and to contextualise media products as appropriate.

This final point is arguably the most challenging area of synopticity in that it requires wider knowledge and understanding. For example, it is fairly easy to look at a 1970s sitcom and regard it in many ways as dated and out of touch with current audience sensitivities, but a synoptic answer will take into account the wider political, social and cultural contexts of 1970s Britain which account for the sitcom being the way it is. It is quite easy to regard a sitcom from the 1970s as not very funny when considering it in the present time but audiences, the nature of comedy and attitudes and values were all very different then from how they are now. The harsh reality here is that you are unlikely to be able to simply acquire these skills of synopticity just by watching or reading your chosen products; you will need to work at them and ask yourself to consider the issues and the contexts which affect the different media you are using in your case study. To help with this, there are a number of key issues, contexts and theories which you might find useful in helping to account for the way media products are.

Issues, contexts and theories which might be applied to case studies for Section B

- Dominant, oppositional and negotiated responses
- Representations and stereotypes
- Media effects
- The world after 9/11 and the role of the media
- Ownership and control
- Regulation and censorship
- Technology and the digital revolution
- Globalisation
- Moral panics
- The role of the media in society
- Semiotics
- Postmodernism
- Colonialism and post-colonialism
- Marxism
- Liberal pluralism
- Gender
- Ethnicity
- Sexuality
- Audience
- The development of genre
- How all of the above have been affected by the passage of time.

Naturally, not all of these will be relevant to your own case studies and so you will need to be selective in deciding which ones are relevant to you. It may be necessary to have a chat with your teacher about this but you can certainly help yourself by being familiar with the main points of each of these contexts and issues as by doing this, their relevance to your case study may become clearer.

You may recognise that this list bears more than a little in common with the theoretical approaches mentioned on pp. 119–20 which might be applied to the case studies in this unit. Indeed, many of the items on this list will have been covered elsewhere in the specification, refer to contexts and debates and have a basis in the key concepts and this is exactly what synopticity is.

Using research in Section B

Your preparation, as we have mentioned earlier, must be thorough and research is likely to have played a major part in your preparation, but this takes many forms and can be done very well or very badly. Good research is illuminating and informative and is the one thing which all students who score the highest marks have done. Research means looking into something or trying to find out an answer, and takes many forms. When you ask some-one for their point of view, this is a form of research, just as reading a text-book, browsing the internet or looking at a media product and drawing your own conclusions are types of research. This unit requires not just secondary research, such as that done with textbooks, TV interviews with media prac-titioners, journals, etc., but also primary research which is you analysing media products and media practices and drawing your own conclusions about them. The box below will help you to distinguish between the two.

Primary research

Primary research is original research, carried out by you, based on the research of others for inspiration, guidance or to form a hypothesis. This may seem like a hard thing to do; it is certainly not something that comes easily to everyone, but that is part of the challenge of advanced study. As you progress to under-graduate and even postgraduate level it becomes even more important. At the very least, you should aim to have an opinion about the matter in hand, be able to discuss the factors which have led to the present situation and to be able to present an informed prediction about its future development (see activity which follows).

Secondary research

Secondary research is what others say about the topic being researched. The deeper you go into a subject and the more skilled you become, the less you tend to rely upon secondary research in your work. Using secondary research is a complicated business. You cannot always be assured of the accuracy or legit-imacy of the work, you will need to acknowledge it lest you are accused of plagiarism and you may even need permission to use it if you are publishing your work.

The main sources of secondary research in the study of media are:

- textbooks
- newspaper or magazine articles
- the internet
- documentaries or interviews
- extras on a DVD such as a 'making of . . .' special.

You are in something of a grey area with MEST3; there is certainly the need to include good quality secondary research in your work and to use it to back up and explain the points you make, but do not completely rely upon it or present it as proof of something. However, you shouldn't omit it altogether as this gives the impression that you are trying to 'wing it' without acknowledging the expert opinions and conclusions of media writers and professionals. A well-balanced A2 answer will include a number of perspectives and points of view and a wide range of sources (do not limit your research to the internet!) and will include both primary and secondary research.

Activity

This activity is designed to get you considering how to use primary research in a meaningful way. Choose one of these six topics, ideally one which you already know a little about.

- The decline in newspaper sales
- Music and film/DVD piracy
- Social networking sites and their impact upon privacy
- Representations of homosexuals in the media
- The increase in the use of digital technology in film and TV special effects
- The proliferation of musical talent shows.

Now consider your response to these four questions. Write down your answers if you wish.

- What is the current situation regarding your chosen issue?
- How did it get this way?
- What is your informed opinion about the issue?
- What do you foresee happening in the future?

Revision tip

The key to success with primary research is to have an opinion about the issue and to be able to make an informed prediction about future developments. You need to realise that you aren't searching for a definitively and absolutely correct answer; there are few of those in a subject such as media. Rather, you are showing the examiner that you have more than a passing knowledge of the topic in question.

Using your research in the exam is a bit like a builder attending an emergency repair job: you will have a range of materials at your disposal which you have built up through the diligent research into your case study. It will cover a lot of issues and debates which are pertinent to the study, and if you are very well prepared, you will have one or two peripheral issues to discuss which are vaguely related to the subject but perhaps which are more clearly relevant to another area of media. In the same way, the builder attends the job with a toolbox full of items, some of which will certainly be needed for the job whilst others may be needed depending upon the nature of the task. Either way, the builder cannot afford to leave any of the tools behind because, like you, they never know what they will need.

Revision tip

If you haven't already done so, you should determine which of your research is primary and which of it is secondary. Having done this, if you feel that there is a lack of one or the other, and mindful that you need some of both, you should set about plugging this gap.

And so, in the exam this is the case with you. You do not know for sure what you will be asked, what you do know is that you will need to draw upon the material you have put together through your research and use it selectively and appropriately to respond to the question which you have been asked to answer.

A further point to consider here is that by engaging in primary research, by offering your own point of view or interpretation of a media product or in response to some secondary research, giving a reason for your conclusions will help you to achieve a degree of critical autonomy. Since Media Studies is a conceptual subject which rarely deals with absolute right or wrong answers, you should find plenty of opportunities to contribute to the debates which exist in most areas of the subject. All you need to work on is the confidence to do it.

How you will be assessed

At the start of this section, we stated that you will need to make a decision about which question you are going to answer in the examination and that you cannot afford to take too much time making this decision. However, there is a huge difference between making a decision quickly and rushing into it.

The first thing you should do in the examination is to take the time to read each question thoroughly. This may seem an obvious thing to say but it is amazing how many candidates respond to essay questions in such a way as to give the distinct impression that they have not done this. In addition, after reading each question, think for a moment about what you are actually being asked to do. Examination questions usually have an instruction located within them somewhere. This takes many forms and instruction words such as 'analyse', 'assess', 'discuss' and 'evaluate' are common, together with questions which simply ask you 'how', 'why' or 'what'. One question you never see is 'Write as much as you can about . . .' and yet many candidates, rather than focus upon what the question is actually asking them to do, set off and produce an answer which does this very thing. No matter how good the answer, how detailed the response, how numerous and current the examples are and how well written the answer is, it is unlikely to score well if it doesn't actually answer the question or focus upon the realms of the topic.

Some candidates prepare for their examinations by preparing an answer in advance and duplicating it in the exam hall. This is not advisable, primarily because the question you prepare your response for is unlikely to come up exactly as you anticipate. Examiners are known for adding variety to their questions and adopting slightly different angles to the topics. If you produce your answer to the question as you would rather it be asked, then you are likely to score poorly because of the lack of focus on the actual question you have been asked to respond to. All you have demonstrated is that you have a good memory and, sadly, whilst this may be a useful attribute for a person to possess, marks are not awarded for it. Instead, marks are awarded for responses which show that the candidate has adapted their understanding and knowledge and applied it to the question being asked.

Exam tips

- Read each question carefully.
- Be sure you understand exactly what you are being asked to do. If you do not, that question is probably not the best one for you. If you do not fully understand any of the questions, ask yourself which one you understand most. However, having a go at past questions as part of your preparation will help you make more sense of questions.
- Do not pre-prepare an answer prior to the exam.
- Answer the question rather than produce an answer to the question you wish had been asked.
- Make frequent and detailed references to your case study and to media products.
- Be sure you understand the difference between a media product and a media industry.

The rationale behind the examination

All exams at every level are assessments which are designed to test your knowledge and understanding of a given topic, but as you progress through to the more advanced level you now find yourself at, there is the additional aspect to an examination of application of this knowledge. Therefore it is not enough to simply know about the topic, or even to understand it; rather you need to use this knowledge and understanding to respond to the question in the most appropriate way. This is broadly what we said in the earlier section on how you will be assessed.

When considering the rationale behind the examination, you should remember the two main foci of the assessment objectives covered in this unit: knowledge and understanding (AO1) and application of this knowledge and understanding when analysing media products (AO2). Your answer therefore must demonstrate your knowledge and understanding of the content of your case study and show how you can use this to answer the questions set. The information below gives you an idea of what you need to have knowledge and understanding of for a case study for MEST 3.

Knowledge and understanding in a case study

Let us look at some examples of putting this approach into practice and two areas which are popular choices in the topics of identity and new media:

gender identities and social networking websites. The boxes which follow take each of these four areas of the case study and list what you might reasonably be expected to know and understand for it. The first example refers to the representations topic and the second to new/digital media.

Case study 1: media representations of the East End of London

Media products:

- BBC coverage of the 2012 Olympic Games and associated documentaries
- A range of films set in London's East End, both contemporary and historical. Examples might include various adaptations of *Oliver Twist*, *The Krays* (1990), *Harry Brown* (2009) and *The Sweeney* (2012)
- TV and newspaper coverage, especially coverage of events such as the riots of 1981 and 2011
- *Eastenders*, although not necessarily for accuracy!
- East End comedy, such as *Only Fools and Horses*
- *Luther* (BBC).

For each you should know:

- How the people are represented
- How the area is represented
- What stereotypes exist about the people and the area and how they are challenged and reinforced by the representations contained in the product studied.

Wider contexts

Social:

- Crime figures for the boroughs of the East End of London (stereotypically regarded as high)
- Educational achievement in the area (stereotypically regarded as low)
- The 'East End' spirit famously reported upon during the Blitz in World War II
- Ethnic diversity and race relations in the area
- Social composition of the area
- The concept of neighbourhood and local initiatives

Figure 16
Olympic Stadium, London,
2012, UK.

Figure 17
Garford housing estate at
night, East London, UK.

- The role of women in the East End
- East End culture – for example, Pearly Kings and Queens, sing-alongs around the piano, jellied eels, pie and mash.

Political:

- Political support in the East End area
- Political activity
- The influence of extreme political views
- Employment.

Historic:

- The development of the East End over the course of the twentieth century
- Building of social housing in the 1960s leading to council estates and tower blocks
- Redevelopment of the area in the twenty-first century and the impact of the Olympics.

Theoretical:

- Marxism and hegemony
- Pluralism
- Feminism.

Relevant key concepts

Language:

- Narrative structure
- Genre (there is an 'East End gangster' genre of film which developed thanks to films such as *Snatch*, *Gangster No. 1*, *Sexy Beast* and *Lock Stock and Two Smoking Barrels*)
- A semiotic approach to how characters are shown through accent, costume, features, etc.
- Bias, especially in news media and relating to certain areas or sections of communities.

Audience:

- Target audiences
- Effects of consumption upon audiences.

Representation:

- Stereotypes (cockney wide-boys, extended families, immigrant communities, lovable rogues, friendly older people)
- Challenges to these stereotypes
- Dangerous areas and a profusion of knife crime among young people
- Redevelopment and outward investment areas.

Institution:

- The business aspects of media in the East End of London
- Regulation and control (check out what OFCOM have said about coverage of controversial *Eastenders* storylines or the coverage of the 2011 riots)
- Increase in media products featuring the East End of London and their popularity
- The technical aspects of the coverage of the Olympics.

Future developments:

- Further investment?
- Decline?
- Changes in immigration leading to a more or less ethnically diverse population?
- The legacy of the Olympics?
- Decline in East End culture?

Figure 18
Social media apps on an
iPhone 4.

Case study 2: social networking sites

Media products:

A range of websites such as:

- Facebook
- Twitter
- MySpace
- TMZ.

For each you should know:

- What each site does (function)
- How people use the site.

Examples of actual use of websites:

- Racial abuse of celebrities/sports people on Twitter
- Online petitions on Facebook
- Instant communication with TV and radio shows.

Wider contexts

Social:

- Freedom
- Cyber-bullying and abuse
- Greater communication opportunities.

Political:

- Democracy
- Freedom of speech.

Economic:

- Costs to consumers
- Hardware costs
- Effect on other forms of media (newspapers, cinema, etc.)
- Economic benefits of synergy, economies of scale and diversification.

Theoretical:

- Marxism and hegemony
- Structuralism and post-structuralism
- Postmodernism
- Liberal pluralism.

Relevant key concepts

Language (semiotic approach):

- Layout and design
- Use of graphics and images
- Mode of address (formal/informal)
- Use of verbal/non-verbal communication
- Intertextuality.

Audience:

- Target audience
- Actual audience
- Potential audience
- The effects of consumption on the audience
- Patterns of use (regional/gender/ages etc.)
- Globalisation.

Representation:

- How people, places and things are shown on social networking sites
- Self-representation
- Stereotypes.

Institution:

- Ownership and control
- Business dimensions (profits)
- Advertising
- Opportunities for synergy
- Regulation and control
- Security and threats to privacy.

Future developments:

- Proliferation?
- Decline?
- People becoming less active?
- People becoming less socially interactive?
- Increase in cyber-bullying and identity theft?
- Increase in illegal file sharing?
- Greater opportunities for people to communicate on a global scale?

The key to success in this part of the course is to know and understand these aspects of the case study. Remember though that you will not be asked simply to write as much as you can about it, so you must be able to apply this knowledge and understanding as necessary to the question you are being asked; a theme we come back to yet again. This is the rationale of the examination and candidates who not only have the knowledge and understanding required and who can adapt and use it will find themselves in a much better position than those who do not.

Having made frequent references to applying your knowledge to the questions asked, it is perhaps a good time to look at a few questions from previous papers to see how they are worded and how they focus upon certain areas.

Specimen questions

Representations in the media (example questions adapted by the authors):

- Why are stereotypes so commonly used by media producers? (48 marks)
- Even when the media create negative representations, modern-day audiences are too canny to be taken in by them. Discuss. (48 marks)
- Media representations have become increasingly complex. We can no longer consider them in simple terms of positive and negative. Do you agree? (48 marks)
- If a representation is repeated across the media time after time, it eventually becomes widely accepted by audiences. Do you think this is true? (48 marks)

New/digital media (source: www.aqa.org)

- New and digital media offer media institutions different ways of reaching audiences. Consider how and why media institutions are using these techniques. (48 marks)

(Question 6 MEST3, Section B January 2011)

Figure 19
Girl with iPad, looking at Justin Bieber fanclub page on Facebook.

- 'To connect, to create, to share creativity or thought, to discuss, to collaborate, to form groups or to combine with others in mutual interests or passions. If you can't see the point of any of those things, you will not see the point of Facebook' (www.guardian.co.uk). What opportunities and/or disadvantages do new and digital media have for audiences? (48 marks)

    (Question 7 MEST3, Section B January 2011)

- The world first heard about the death of Michael Jackson from the online gossip website TMZ. How has new/digital media changed the ways in which information reaches audiences and what are the implications? (48 marks)

    (Question 6 MEST3, Section B June 2011)

- 'New and digital media erodes the dividing line between reporters and reported, between active producers and passive audiences: people are enabled to speak for themselves' (www.indymedia.org.uk). Have such developments made the media more democratic, with more equal participation by more people? (48 marks)

    (Question 7 MEST3, Section B June 2011)

In analysing these questions, the rationale behind the examination becomes clearer. The examiners are testing your ability to adapt your case study material to the question asked, to discuss the relevant issues and debates and to include wider issues and contexts. In addition, candidates are expected to provide plenty of examples and to refer extensively to the case study. Some of the questions (e.g. the second and third questions in this list of examples) have a focus on a certain aspect of digital media, in this case websites, whilst others (e.g. the first and fourth questions) do not refer to anything specifically.

However, the questions you will be asked in this unit will be open. You could be forgiven for thinking that this is not the case with some of those listed here but if you look closely at those questions which seem to refer to specific media examples, Facebook and TMZ, you are not actually being asked to refer exclusively to these in your answer; they are just being used to lay a foundation for the context of the question. In actual fact, all four of these questions provide the freedom to discuss whichever examples of digital and new media you wish. This is further evidence of the need to spend time studying the question, as a cursory glance may suggest that you need to focus upon specific areas, and students who have not researched either of these two websites might be discouraged from attempting these questions. But if you have embarked upon a case study which deals, for example, with the impact of digital and new media on the news media and incorporates a study of the decline of newspaper sales and the provision of online news media, then you are indeed well placed to answer the third question, despite its reference to TMZ, as it actually refers to the way audiences receive information, which is, and will continue to be, a key debate in the area of news media. There will be a choice of two questions on each topic and in addition to your knowledge and understanding, part of the skill of being a successful advanced level student is the ability to differentiate quickly between the questions and to respond to the one which gives you the opportunity to construct your best response.

The essay response

The word essay has the capacity to strike fear into the hearts of students, and especially among those whose strengths lie more in the practical aspects of a subject. Many students find the freedom that practical coursework affords more to their liking. Obviously, there is less of a time constraint since final deadlines are frequently months in advance and numerous opportunities exist for reworking, re-editing and even wholesale changes, whereas an essay, under examination conditions, is planned, written and checked over (in this case) in only an hour, and presents much more of a challenge to most people. However, perhaps it is time to rethink this maligned method of assessment.

At the risk of becoming even more clichéd, there are certain similarities between other experiences in life and an essay. There are obvious parallels with things such as going to an audition or an interview: a single chance to impress followed by a sense of success or failure, but as with those reality TV contestants and job applicants, preparation is the key.

Preparation is itself something which requires thought and cannot be entered into lightly, because flawed preparation will inevitably lead to a flawed outcome. A driver setting off on a new journey (let us for the moment imagine that there is no satellite navigation or GPS available and a good old-fashioned map must be relied upon) will need to plan a route. Failure to plan the route won't mean that the driver fails to arrive at the destination – even the least geographically aware driver will probably make it eventually, but the journey will be fraught, the wrong direction will be taken, dead ends encountered; the journey will not be made gracefully or economically, and it is unlikely that the driver will arrive on time.

Now consider the student in an exam hall in the same position. Without a good plan, mistakes will be made, important information may be missed out whilst other pieces of information are repeated. The lack of a plan may mean that you make a point about X then move onto Y before realising that you haven't said all there is to say about X and so you go back, rather like the unprepared driver going round in circles.

In many ways, an essay is like a journey. There are many routes to take but some are better than others. Well-answered essays require economy and style. Points need to flow, and the response should have a structure. Some teachers encourage a Point, Evidence, Explain (PEE) approach, which might be adopted if the question is appropriate. You will doubtlessly have an introduction and a conclusion to the essay but there are many ways to approach writing an answer. We will look later at more specific ways to tackle the questions but for now, rather than regard an essay as an awkward assessment which you are not looking forward to, try to convince yourself that your exams are a chance to show off, to show the examiner just how good you are, to demonstrate how much you know and understand and how well you can adapt your knowledge to overcome the obstacle they have put in front of you. Above all, set out to put the examiner in a corner, one in which they feel that they have no other alternative than to award you high marks.

Of course, all of this depends upon the quality of the preparation, the depth of the case study and the amount of practice you have undertaken prior to entering the exam hall.

There is a temptation to prepare a specimen answer in advance of the exam which you will learn and reproduce but we have already warned against this approach. Once again, it is worth reiterating the dangers with it: you are most likely to answer the question you have prepared for rather than the question which you are actually being asked and so, at best, your response will veer into irrelevance and show a lack of focus; at worst you will not answer the question asked at all. Nevertheless, it is a very smart move to produce

Exam tips

- Take time to read and re-read the question.
- Take time to consider what you are actually being asked to do.
- Highlight any keywords which you will need to keep in mind as you write your essay.
- Complete a plan. There are several ways to do this: you might make some notes, do a flowchart or complete a spider diagram. Give yourself plenty of space for your plan so that you can add things to it as you go along.
- Remember to get the balance between critical autonomy (which can be achieved through referring to your primary research, reference to a range of examples and some reference to relevant theories and secondary research).
- Manage your time. This way you can see whether you are going to finish within the time limit or overrun.
- If you do run out of time, try to realise this before the end of the exam. If necessary, stop 'writing' your answer and begin to bullet point your last points – it is better to do this than to continue writing and not say everything you wanted to.
- Try to incorporate some time for checking your answer.

answers to past questions so that you can practise the approach to take and ensure that there is the correct balance between your primary and secondary research. Past questions represent an excellent way to revise as well.

Answering the question

In the exam tips box above, advice for answering the question is offered. Let us take a look at two of the sample questions from the January 2011 paper again to illustrate what this means:

- New and digital media offer media institutions different ways of reaching audiences. Consider how and why media institutions are using these techniques.
- 'To connect, to create, to share creativity or thought, to discuss, to collaborate, to form groups or to combine with others in mutual interests or passions. If you can't see the point of any of those things, you will not see the point of Facebook' (www.guardian.co.uk). What opportunities and/or disadvantages do new and digital media have for audiences?

Somewhere within your answer to either one of these questions there are certain things that must be included. For the first one, you cannot simply reproduce the material you have researched in your case study. Your answer must say how and why media institutions are using the techniques the question refers to. Similarly, for the second question, the answer must contain reference to the opportunities and the disadvantages new and digital media have for audiences. It is expected that having asked these specific questions, an answer is offered, even if that answer is little more than an opinion – which is actually to be encouraged if it is an informed opinion based upon evidence.

Suggestions for writing an essay answer

- Decode the question. You may be instructed to do certain things:

  - analyse
  - assess
  - discuss
  - compare
  - evaluate
  - or you may be asked a direct question as is the case with the sample questions we have been looking at.

- Break the essay into chunks.
- Begin with an introduction in which you outline the context of the essay and define any key terms from within the question. In your introduction, try to make the examiner realise that you are confident and that you know what you are doing.
- In the main body of the essay, make points backed up with explanations and evidence, which will usually be examples, and try to make them flow. Adopt a logical approach with all points of view from one side together followed by alternative viewpoints, or one point followed by an alternative point before then going back. You should also make sure that all points of view are acknowledged and even though it is fine to have a personal bias, you should try to be impartial when weighing up evidence. So if you think that the emergence of new and digital media heralds the end of traditional print news media and that this is a good thing, there are enough people involved in the media who do not share these points of view, and so this position must be present in your discussion. You should aim in the main body of your answer to make about four main points, each with evidence or an explanation and examples.

- Conclude your essay at the end and summarise the main points you have made. If there is a direct question to answer on the balance of a discussion, then the conclusion would be a good place to offer the answer. It is also the ideal place to allow your own points of view to prevail, so long as you can justify them.
- Learn important connective terms and phrases such as:

  - furthermore
  - however
  - in addition
  - alternatively
  - nevertheless
  - on the whole
  - on balance.

- Focus upon spelling, punctuation and grammar. Well-structured and articulate answers are rewarded.

How to revise for Section B

Hopefully by now you will have realised that advanced examinations are not simply a test of what you know, or more specifically what you can remember in an exam. This is especially so with this exam. It is the way you use your knowledge and understanding to respond to the question you are answering that is the main focus of this section of MEST3. Having said that, there are certain things you need to know and which therefore should be learned. As we have discussed before, it is all about being prepared in case you need a certain piece of knowledge, and so the following list is a suggestion of what you may need to know in the exam. Do not limit yourself to this list: there may be other items which are needed depending upon the case study you have chosen.

- It goes without saying that you need to know detailed information based upon your case study. This includes key technological developments (e.g. keeping in touch with people through social networking sites or downloading news on your mobile phone is only possible because of the huge technological advances in recent years, both in hardware and software), the main players (companies, regulators, individuals) in your case study, developments over time in terms of use and application, example materials, etc.

- Relevant theoretical approaches such as Marxism, hegemony, pluralism, semiotics, gender and ethnicity theories, media effects models.
- One or two key quotes which you might use to illustrate your points. At least you should be able to paraphrase what certain key people or authors have said or written.
- Analysis techniques.

However, as we approach this crucial question of what to revise, and this is really something which your own case study dictates, we are also faced with the equally crucial question of *how* to revise. There is a wide array of academic work which has been undertaken all over the world on how people study and how they best revise. A good place to begin in addressing this is to ask yourself what kind of a learner you are. Active learners who are self-motivated, who possess enquiring minds and who don't rely on their teachers, classmates or a search engine make the best students in subjects such as media and, hopefully, you are one of these. However, that doesn't address what kind of learner you are.

So what type of learner are you? Maybe you are a 'listener' and you prefer to learn through what you hear. On the other hand, you may be a 'looker' and find that seeing is the best way for you to learn. Alternatively, you may be a 'doer', someone who finds completing practical tasks are the best way. Some students – perhaps they are the lucky ones – can utilise sight, sound *and* activity to learn depending upon the task but, generally, people tend to fall predominantly into one of these categories as a preferred learning style. The following box looks more closely at the learning styles of these three types of student.

Listeners, known as auditory learners

Learning style

Auditory learners take in a lot of information in the classroom from what the teacher and other students say. They are able to recollect spoken information from DVD and TV clips.

Revision techniques

These might include:

- Speaking to the teacher and other students
- Recording revision notes onto an MP3 player to listen back

- Making up rhymes and sayings about topics
- Repeating things to themselves.

Lookers, known as visual learners

Learning style

The main sources of learning for visual learners are from visual stimuli, especially books/magazines/newspapers and the images, pictures and written text they contain. Like auditory learners, visual learners can find TV, DVD or live performance useful.

Revision techniques

These might include:

- Producing flowcharts, graphs and diagrams
- Reading through notes.

Doers, known as kinaesthetic learners

Learning style

Kinaesthetic learners learn best through activity and are naturally perhaps more suited to the practical aspects of media studies than the academic. They retain much more information from first-hand practical experience than from reading and listening.

Revision techniques

These might include:

- Producing sticky notes with the main revision pointers on
- Rewriting class notes into revision notes
- Organising physical notes into categories linked to the topic being revised.

You will probably recognise yourself in one of these categories more than the other two. However, whichever you find the most effective for your own learning and revision, there is a certain amount of information of a general media nature and linked to your own case study which you will need to have at your disposal for this exam, and so one way or another you will need to learn it. Your teacher or tutor will be able to advise you more on learning styles.

What makes a good case study?

There is of course the expectation here that you have completed a good and detailed case study in the area of either 'representations in the media' or 'the impact of new/digital media' which will form the foundation of your response. Flawed case studies will most likely lead to a low-quality answer since the subject about which you are responding – your case study – is of a low quality. Perhaps now is a good time to consider your case study in more depth. We have already discussed what topics you might investigate for your case study but there are a few other considerations which you should be aware of in terms of not just producing any old case study, but making it a good one.

In addition to getting advice from your teachers, who know you well and can advise on your own particular ideas, it's a good idea to look towards the awarding body for more general advice. Examination past questions, mark schemes and examiners' reports are available for downloading from the AQA website, so browsing through these pages in order to see first hand what the awarding body are looking for is time well spent as you prepare for the examination.

www.aqa.org

Advice regarding case studies

Naturally, since all students are unique and have their own particular interests and skills, offering general advice is something best done in conjunction with advice you receive from your teacher or lecturer but in general the best case studies are characterised by certain common features.

A variety of media products from within the three media platforms is essential to demonstrate that you have breadth of knowledge. There are many different approaches to a case study, as we have seen in the earlier suggestions for case studies, and the best case studies will be replete with a variety of different media products reflecting different producers, ideologies and functions.

Good case studies also have plenty of detail and depth and you should have lots of examples which provide evidence that you have researched around the particular topic or product and engaged with the wider contextual aspects. In good responses, theory is used wisely to augment the case study and to either reinforce or challenge the points you make.

Finally, examiners are always happy to get a sense of the enthusiasm and interest you have in the areas covered by the case studies you have chosen. Your engagement, or conversely your lack of engagement, will be evident to an examiner, so if it hasn't already dawned upon you that you would be advised to choose case studies which appeal to your interests, it certainly should have done.

These few simple pieces of advice should be used as a checklist for your case study; we have already looked in this section at the wisdom of using a wide range of products and examples, awareness of media debates and the use of theory to support your work. However, engagement with the case study is something we have not really discussed.

This piece of advice suggests that a student's genuine interest and enthusiasm for a topic tend to shine through and that the issues discussed and formulation of opinion are more thorough and of a higher quality. It also makes sense that if you are engaging in a case study which is likely to take some months to complete, you choose a topic about which you are interested or have a desire to research further, not least because your enthusiasm should spur you on. The months spent on your case study will be long indeed if your interest in the topic you have chosen is minimal.

What makes a good answer?

Producing a good-quality answer is difficult in a subject such as media which seldom has a definitive right or wrong answer. Your job, as we have suggested before, is to impress the examiner and to show off what you know. Ideally you will have been studying and immersing yourself in a wide range of debates, theories and primary-based research associated with your chosen area of study, often alone or perhaps on occasions with other members of the class, so now it's only natural that you should want to show off and let the world rather than just your teacher realise just how much you know. Clearly you will need to be well-versed in your case study, to have researched thoroughly and to be able to draw upon appropriate theories and wider contexts. However, subject knowledge, the prime motivator behind a good-quality answer, can be undermined if you do not write your answer well. You will need to write in an engaging manner with plenty of relevant examples and with good quality spelling and punctuation in evidence throughout. Hopefully this final point is not something you think of entirely as in the remit of Key Stage 2 and 3 English lessons – you spend time on spelling and punctuation at these levels so that you can express yourself fluently and with style both in English and elsewhere in the curriculum, and indeed for the rest of your life. Now is not the time to adopt a 'spelling and grammar don't matter' attitude – they are life skills and your examiners will be looking for you to demonstrate good skills in this area.

And you must answer the question which is being asked rather than write the answer you would prefer to write.

Writing an answer in an essay is a little like a job interview in that your success or failure can come down to, after planning and preparation – not to mention nerves and the occasional bout of panic – a simple task. Like an interview, you will not know in advance the questions which you will be asked, but you will have a general idea about the areas they will cover. This is especially so in your examination since although the questions are based upon the topics you have researched, you cannot be sure of exactly what you will be asked.

So, the key is to prepare and to practise writing answers under exam conditions. Although your teacher is likely to ask you to do this as part of the formal class-based preparation, there is nothing to stop you from trying it yourself when you have a spare hour and teachers are likely to be willing to mark the work for you. Again, whilst we do not recommend the preparation of a 'stock' answer, there is a lot to be gained from using sample questions in terms of knowledge of the topic – they are a useful revision tool – and also in your style of writing.

A look at a mark scheme on the awarding body's website will reveal exactly what the examiners were looking for on the past papers for the best marks, so it is a very good idea to seek these out and to use them as revision aids. Generally, examiners are looking for a comprehensive and detailed discussion of the relevant points and for candidates to show understanding of the topic they are being asked to write about. It should go without saying that you should be focused on the question and although it is fine to discuss wider issues, you will need to actually answer the question you are being asked.

Top answers will use theory effectively. They will also engage in the wider contexts, which cover historical, cultural and social contexts, incorporate any relevant debates, either current or historical, and have a sense of critical autonomy in which your own points of view emerge and are justified evidentially. One of these points of view may well be based upon a kind of prediction about the future – consideration of further developments will always be welcome as long as the prediction is plausible, so have an informed opinion about what might happen in the future and be prepared to argue it. The response will use a wide variety of appropriate examples and as a second year advanced student, experienced in responding to essay answers in examination conditions having done it so many times before, there is an expectation in the top answers for clarity, articulation and sophisticated writing found in a well-structured response.

The first question many students often ask when considering their response to an examination question refers to the length of the answer. If you have ever asked this question to one of your teachers, you will most likely have been told something like it is quality rather than quantity which counts, and this is true. Having said that, you are unlikely to score well if you have written two sides or less, but ten sides suggests a lack of depth and detail. The amount of paper used also depends upon the size of the student's writing. The average student writes around 300 to 350 words on a side of A4 paper so based upon that, three sides will be around 900 to 1050 words. As a rough guide, you should aim for between three and four sides which, given the fact that you have an hour to respond, means spending about 12 minutes per side which will also allow you some time for planning and reading through your work.

Going back to the advice your teacher is likely to have given you, it is true that a quality response is required and this, more than any other factor, is what should be your guide as you prepare for the MEST3 Section B examination and which should lead you to conclude that your best preparation for the exam is to revise, attempt past questions and to know the details of your case study inside out.

PART 4

AFTER THE EXAM

HOW EXAMS ARE MARKED

Once you have been told to stop writing and your exam script has been collected by the invigilator, that may be the end of the process for you. All you have then is the nervous wait of a few weeks until you get your result. For the awarding bodies which set and mark exams, that period between the end of the exam and the results deadline will be one of frenzied activity to ensure that all students get their grade on time. This is obviously especially important if you have a place at university riding on the outcome of your exam.

We thought you might find it useful if we gave you an idea of precisely what happens to your exam script once you have completed the exam. The marking of all papers within a GCE unit, such as MEST1 or MEST3, is under the control of a principal examiner. The principal examiner, who is the most senior examiner responsible for an individual unit, is given the final say in determining the marks that each candidate will receive. As he or she cannot mark every question on every single paper individually, the principal examiner is supported by a large number of other examiners so that the marking process can be completed in time for everyone to get their result. This means that there has to be some way of ensuring that all examiners are marking the script of every candidate to the same standard as the principal examiner.

This process of ensuring fair and accurate marking of each candidate's script is called standardisation. What happens in this process is that the principal examiner selects a sample of scripts from those written by students taking the unit for which he or she is responsible and uses these scripts to set the marking standards. The principal examiner does this by giving the questions on each script a mark and explaining to the rest of the examining team how each mark awarded has been arrived at. Each examiner must then have a go at a test of their own by marking a number of scripts, using the mark scheme and the sample of the principal examiner's scripts as guidelines. If their marks are accurate, they will be allowed to continue marking the scripts allocated to them. If not, they may have to mark a further sample of script or even be stopped from marking altogether.

NOTE

In a large subject such as Media Studies with many thousands of candidates entered, the principal examiner will be supported by a team of senior examiners who will help by checking each examiner's marking at different stages of the marking process to ensure that they remain accurate in their assessment of scripts. The examiners themselves are organised into a hierarchy with the principal examiner at the top. He or she will be supported by senior examiners, also known as team leaders. Each team leader will supervise a team of examiners to make sure that they are marking each script accurately.

Almost all the exam marking process for all subjects is now carried out online. Instead of marking your actual paper script, an examiner is now likely to be asked to mark a scan of part of it on his or her computer screen. There are some important implications of this for you. First, because an examiner will mark just one question from your script rather than all of it, several different examiners will each mark one individual question that you have answered. It is therefore very important that you focus specifically on the individual question you are being asked as the examiner can no longer see your whole paper. The implication of this is that if you have got the wrong response in the wrong place, the examiner can no longer make any allowance for this. Obviously as a candidate it is in your interests to be as precise as you can in responding to each of the individual questions. For example, in MEST1 Section A, your response to a question about Media Audiences should clearly focus on that particular concept. Avoid getting confused – for example, by writing information that belongs under the heading of Media Representations. You won't get any credit for it.

Second, you should make every effort to ensure that your response is as neat and well organised as possible. Reading handwriting on a computer monitor is a lot easier for the examiner if you have taken care to use a decent quality pen and tried to write with clarity. Using paragraphs, where appropriate, also helps the process.

After all the scripts have been marked, each student's marks will have been recorded and entered into the awarding body's database. These marks will then be used to calculate the grade you receive for that individual unit. Your marks for each of the units, including the coursework units, are then used to calculate the grade you receive for either your AS or A2 qualification as a whole.

In the next section we explain what you need to do if you don't think the grade you have been given fairly reflects your achievement in any of the units.

WHAT IF YOU ARE NOT HAPPY WITH YOUR GRADE?

If, when you receive your results, you are not happy with your grade, there are procedures you can follow to make sure that your paper has been marked accurately and fairly. However, you can only instigate these checking procedures through your school or college; it is not possible for you to arrange directly to have your paper re-marked. This can only be done with the agreement of your school/college. You will also find that there is a financial implication here, that is, it is going to cost money. Whether you pay yourself or the school agrees to foot the bill is something you may need to argue about but it is worth bearing in mind that the cost of getting your paper checked properly is in the region of £40.

Of course getting your script re-marked would come at the worst possible time, when you are waiting to see if you have been accepted for a university place or are going through the clearing process to see what places may be available to someone with your grades. Acting swiftly and deciding what to do is therefore essential.

Wherever possible, enlist the support of your Media Studies teacher in the process. Your teacher will be able to advise you about how realistic your chances are of getting your grade changed.

The first thing to do is to get a copy of your exam script for the unit you are concerned about. You need to do this through your school's exams office. Be sure that your teacher will be available to look at the script with you and tell you if he or she thinks you have been marked fairly or not. If your school believes on the evidence of your script that your grade is unfair, you can then go to the stage of getting a re-mark.

> **NOTE**
>
> Your school may decide on the evidence of your script that other students may also have been marked unfairly, in which case they may ask to have several, or even all, candidates who entered the unit to be re-marked.

This means that your script will be re-marked by a senior examiner to check that the mark you have received is accurate and fair. The awarding body will also check that the marks you received have been added up correctly and transferred to the database accurately. If the senior examiner's marks indicate that your grade for the unit should be changed, then the awarding body will make the necessary change and let you know.

If you are told that no change will be made to your grade and you and your school remain convinced that you deserve a better grade, you still have the right to take the matter to appeal with the awarding body. They will send out a report of the re-mark that they undertook and consider your appeal at an in-house committee.

When you receive the result of your appeal, you still have a further option to take your appeal to the Examinations Appeal Board (EAB). The EAB will let you know if they are prepared to listen to your appeal and if they agree to do so, a hearing will be arranged before their panel. Obviously you and your teacher will have to feel that you have a very good case for a grade change if you take your case as far as this.

NOTE

All these procedures have to be conducted to tight deadlines, both in terms of your request for a re-mark and the response of the awarding body, so make sure you are aware of all the crucial deadlines. You can get these either from your school's exams office or directly from the AQA website.

RESOURCES

Essential media sites

- BBC Radio 4's *The Media Show* is an easily accessible and extremely useful way of keeping up to date with contemporary issues and debates. This weekly half hour show is essential listening for students who want to be at the cutting edge of the world of the media. Probably the best way to listen is through BBC iPlayer, as there are nearly 200 programmes archived on the site. You can download the programme and listen at your convenience.

    Presented by Steve Hewlitt, a journalist and former TV executive, the programme features 'the latest stories and opinion from the fast-changing world of media in all its forms – print, television, radio, online and telecommunications'.

Detailed information about current and archived programmes can be found on www.bbc.co.uk/ podcasts/series/media.

- The *Guardian* has a special area of its website which is devoted to the media, Media Guardian. This is essential reading for media students as it covers news stories and has features which give you an excellent insight into the contemporary media industry.

    Within Media Guardian there are sections dedicated to different media industries: radio, advertising, press, digital media, TV, the music industry. Each of these provides coverage of contemporary media issues within the relevant industry, making them excellent resources for Section B of the exam at AS and A2. By following Media Guardian on Twitter you will receive regular links to recent developments in the media industry.

    The website also has an extensive multimedia site on mainstream, independent and art cinema featuring interviews with directors, producers and actors and analysis of trends in the contemporary film industry.

www.guardian.co.uk/ media

- MediaKnowall is a really useful comprehensive site, which includes plenty of resources specifically for A level. The resources cover the media concepts as well as a range of topic areas, which would be really useful for researching wider contexts and critical perspectives.

www.mediaknowall.com

Websites for wider reference

- All the national press have film websites: www.telegraph.co.uk/culture/film/ and www.independent.co.uk/arts-entertainment/ are particularly worth exploring.

www.timewarner.com/our-content

www.nbcuni.com/

- An easy way to study the structure of multimedia global corporations is to explore their websites (this should be used as research for institutions rather than as a media product). Good examples include Time Warner and NBC Universal.

www.adnative.net

- Adnative is the website of a network of media sales professionals which produces a monthly newsletter that you can subscribe to for free and is emailed directly. The newsletter includes media news, especially media institution news, from around the world.

www.bbc.co.uk

- BBC online offers you not only the opportunity to catch up on any BBC programmes missed over the past week but also to find out more about what the BBC does and how it is organised. A really useful resource.

www.boxofficemojo.com

- Box Office Mojo, like the Internet Movie Database (imdb) (its parent company), is a database of information about films and the wider film industry. Box Office Mojo has a more detailed business focus than imdb, providing breakdowns of film budgets, box office, release schedules and marketing campaigns. Information such as the takings for domestic (US) box office in comparison to foreign takings for each film gives a useful insight into the position of contemporary Hollywood. Although the focus is the Hollywood film industry the site covers cinema exhibition worldwide.

http://collider.com/

- Collider.com is a site covering 'Movies, television, gadgets, sports, video games – anything of interest to the media and technology-savvy individual.' The emphasis on covering 'breaking news' across the media and technology industries means that it covers the different stages of distribution (for films and games in particular) in great detail, providing a handy archive for links to teaser campaigns, trailers, scavenger hunts, fan forums, etc.

www.imdb.com

- The Internet Movie Database for everything to do with film, release dates, budgets, filming locations, cast lists, biographies, etc. The site also includes TV shows.

www.indiewire.com

- IndieWire, as the name suggests, focuses on independent filmmaking, covering all aspects of independent distribution and exhibition. Although it is a US site, it features global independent film culture. More recently indiewire has also covered developments in the TV industry with a particular interest in Web-based TV programming.

www.pressgazette.co.uk

- Press Gazette has a wealth of information about the magazine and newspaper industries including circulation figures, articles and discussions.

www.screenonline.org.uk/

- Screenonline is an educational website which is steadily building a comprehensive archive for British film and television. Really useful, and very accessible and interesting.

- Theory.org is a website operated by David Gauntlett of the University of Westminster and is based upon social and cultural theory. It contains an array of information about identity and representations among other useful material.

www.theory.org.uk

Media regulation websites

It is a good idea to keep up to date with any websites of regulatory bodies that have specific relevance to the industries you have explored. These include the PCC for the newspaper industry, ASA for advertising and the BBFC for film classification. We have also added something on the regulation of video games and music.

- The Advertising Standards Authority is the regulator of advertising across the UK. Very informative and well-presented website.

www.asa.org.uk

- The British Board of Film Classification has an excellent website and is the independent body that classifies all UK film releases.

www.bbfc.co.uk

- Ofcom is the independent regulator of British broadcasting. Its website is a very comprehensive source for finding out about what it does and issues affecting contemporary British broadcasting.

www.ofcom.org.uk

- The Video Standards Council is the designated body responsible for the age-rating of video games.

www.videostandards. org.uk

Subscription sites

MediaMagazine is published – online or in traditional format – with A level media students in mind. If you subscribe, you have access to an archive of past issues. It is highly recommended for both AS and A2 media students.

www.englishandmedia. co.uk/mm/index.html

MediaEdu is a useful subscription site for Media Studies. Check with your teacher if it is possible to get access.

http://media.edusites. co.uk/

CONCLUSION

We hope that you have found this book useful and that it will help you to achieve the grade you feel you deserve in your Media Studies exam.

One question you may be asking yourself as you pore over your textbooks and voraciously consume media products in preparation for your exam is: is this all worthwhile? For many students, GCE Media Studies is the beginning of a lifelong adventure into the media. The production work you completed at AS or the essay you wrote at A2 may well become a defining moment in your life, well beyond the narrow confines of getting a decent A-level grade. Many students so enjoy the work they have undertaken in the GCE Media Studies that for them it becomes a career path that can lead to a lifetime of work in the media and its related industries. For others it might well be just an interesting experience, although it is worth bearing in mind that many of the skills you have developed in your course of study will benefit you whatever career you choose to pursue.

We thought, therefore, that an interesting way to conclude this book would be to ask a former GCE Media Studies student, Steven Prior, to tell you himself just where his GCE Media Studies course finally led. Steven is currently working as an assistant producer in the television industry. Here is his response to our questions.

A brief outline of your media education would be helpful.

My formal media education began at sixth form where I studied Media Studies at both AS Level and A Level. The course was fully theoretical and was my first detailed study of the many different forms of media and how they work. With the subject not available to me at GCSE level, I was instead able to satisfy my curiosity at this time with short work experience stints at local TV and radio stations and hospital radio.

Following A Levels I enrolled on a BA degree in Media Production at the University of Lincoln. This three-year course was equally split between media theory and practical elements and it was then that I was finally able to gain practical experience of broadcast standard technical equipment. As the course progressed we narrowed down and selected the disciplines we wished to pursue through to our final year, which involved producing coursework relevant to each. On the academic side, we always had essays – and in the final year a dissertation – to accompany and complement the coursework.

Any defining moments in your media education – topics, teachers, discoveries that set your soul on fire?

At sixth form I had a terrific Media Studies teacher who really made the subject come alive in ways that other tutors simply could not. There was a clear passion on her behalf and along with her ability to spark an open debate and discussion within each topic we addressed meant we couldn't help but engage with the material. Suffice to say Media Studies lessons were among the liveliest and most interesting I was involved with during my time at college.

Further down the line at university, on the practical side of the course we were encouraged to form our own working teams. I consider myself incredibly lucky to have worked within the team I did because each of us were really committed to producing the best standard of coursework possible but in such different ways. Within our team of six, there was one guy who was a mature student and had worked as a screenwriter for a number of years and he had come back to 'retrain' as a video editor. Because of his previous experience of actually working in the industry, within our group he naturally assumed the role of what would be called the 'show runner' within the TV industry. He would encourage and steer us in certain directions but in a way that allowed us to be creative and feel confident when putting forward our own ideas. When you are in that sort of environment, the creative freedom this allows only serves to encourage and drive you towards making the absolute most of the situation you are in.

In our final year we had the freedom to completely write and produce our own short films. Within our team of six we quickly decided on individual roles: the writers set about writing the short story; this was then broken down by the producer, which was then used by the director as his basis for the casting sessions, which then allowed the art department (one person) to think about costume and locations to film. The short film was originally set in Las Vegas and we had aspirations of raising funds to travel over to the US to shoot it all on the Strip. This was soon scaled back to Soho in London due to not securing any funding at all! However, we believed we still had a good story and went into production.

We held casting sessions and rehearsals, hired camera equipment, arranged relevant filming permissions and it was all a great challenge – we started to feel like filmmakers. At the time, it did set our souls on fire; it made a career in the media seem incredibly attractive, as if it was the only thing we would ever wish to do from there. And what could be better than spending your time being challenged in these uniquely creative ways? Out of the six of us in our group, five are now working full time in careers in the media.

How do you see the relationship between 'theory', or the more academic aspects of the discipline, and production skills? How useful do you think are the production skills that you develop at GCE and undergraduate level?

Honestly, the relationship can be whatever you choose to make of it. From experience of both the practical and the theoretical elements at A Level and degree level, it always felt like an obvious decision to pursue the production side. The theory is useful in that it grounds your practical work, allows you to apply the same analytical methods to your own work as you would when analysing other media output – for example, when thinking about influences or a certain style of filmmaking.

In the work I do now as an assistant producer within the television industry, the practical skills are of most use. The way this industry is changing means that roles are merging, and we are encouraged to develop technical, journalistic and interpersonal skills. For example, an assistant producer will often be required to shoot large parts of documentary films as well as identifying the stories, characters and locations with which to explore the subject. The production skills developed at undergraduate level were extremely useful, not just through how I can directly apply them to the technical requirements of my work now but also through the thrill and enjoyment that characterised a key part of my education and encouraged me to pursue a career in this field.

Did academic Media Studies ever appeal to you as a career option? Or were you sold on production?

I was always sold on production. As soon as we finished our final year, I couldn't wait to start job hunting while the skills and experiences were still fresh in my mind. I had enjoyed everything I had done on the practical side so much that it was only ever in my mind to try to apply this to a career doing the same. I guess I was keen to use that enthusiasm and make the most of it while it lasted because I understood how daunting a task it is to suddenly be thrust out into the world and have to find your place within it.

How easy was it to get a media job? Maybe you could outline the process by which you got your first media job.

Not easy at all. As soon as I left university – or even while I was still there – I started contacting production companies to enquire about work experience or entry-level roles such as intern or runner. I had no luck. I put together a CV and would send this around to as many email addresses as I could find as well as personally visiting offices of production companies.

After months of searching, I came across a large company called RDF who are a big player in the TV industry. They have a much sought-after runner internship that I applied for but initially failed. After saying they would keep me in mind, they offered me work transcribing footage for some of their programmes. The disappointment subsided as I realised that although I wasn't there yet, I had got my foot in the door at a successful TV company. This work lasted three weeks and allowed me to at least meet some of the people working in the industry and get a rough sense of how things worked. After those three weeks, they took me on as a runner and things took off from there.

Can you give us a brief summary of your current job in the media? An example of a typical day (if one exists) might be helpful. What are you most pleased to have achieved? Are there any memorable moments? Any you would prefer to forget?

My current position is assistant producer but can also be referred to as shooting AP or DV director depending on the specific requirements of the role. I am a freelancer, which means I am employed on fixed-term contracts and typically hired after a show has been green lit or commissioned by a broadcaster and for an agreed number of weeks or the duration for which the show is scheduled to be 'in production'.

The role of an assistant producer is not an entry level position but comes from roughly four or five years' experience in the industry, working through from runner and researcher. My genre of television is factual entertainment and I tend to focus on observational documentaries within that field. An AP is responsible for finding and identifying stories, and finding key contributors to tell those stories, but can also be responsible for filming the content or even directing key parts of programming. Depending on the production, an AP tends to work under the producer/director but has a key role to play in how the story is captured and portrayed.

A typical day in the office would most likely be spent conducting background research, finding contributors or planning shoots. Research could be into the storylines the programme is following or fleshing out interesting ways to look at the issues involved. Identifying contributors for the show involves exploring why they are relevant to the subject matter and if they are able to articulate this in front of the camera. Planning and setting up a location shoot would mean writing up a detailed schedule, arranging filming permissions at each location or confirming transport arrangements.

On location the role is likely to include briefing contributors on the topics or talking points and ensuring that the filming runs smoothly through management of runners/researchers. A shooting AP will be required to film all or parts of the items needed from that location, often working alone or under the guidance of a director or producer.

How useful do you think your employers find the skills you developed as part of your media education? How big a culture shift was it from education to actually doing the job?

I think the skills developed through media education are important but not the first thing an employer looks for. The most relevant things at my level are experience and skills developed on the job as well as how you can sell your abilities and ideas in an interview situation. For those starting out and looking for entry-level positions, experience is less important. It becomes more about your attitude, enthusiasm and willingness.

Employers understand that skills learnt early on in an applicant's media education will have given them a fantastic opportunity to develop and hone their abilities but also that the most useful experience comes on the job. The role of runner often gets a bad reputation for exploiting keen individuals but in my opinion it is the perfect way for someone who is new to the industry to see how things work, see which roles appeal to them and what areas of programming they wish to pursue. It is also important to remember that almost every person working in any role in TV has been a runner at the start of his or her career.

The shift from education to working in the industry was not what I expected. First, it took a lot longer than I envisaged it would to get my foot in the door. As a final year media student you are used to being free to work up your ideas and having power and control over them. This doesn't disappear altogether when starting work but it can come as a shock to see your creativity somewhat temporarily curtailed by the urgency to execute your duties, which are likely to include making teas and coffees, delivering packages and labelling tapes.

How do you respond to those who dismiss Media Studies as a frivolous and 'easy' subject at school and university?

I think the idea that Media Studies is an easy subject is very out of date. The role of the media has become far more important over the past ten years and is therefore much more relevant in all facets of society. As it continues to grow there is more reason to analyse and study it and understand the many different ways media affects our lives. It is also easy to dismiss new and less traditional subjects as frivolous just because their origins don't extend as far back as core subjects such as English, Maths or the Sciences. Comparatively the products used in Media Studies could be considered modern in relation to those studied for an English degree, but why should that mean the subject is easier?

I think in the current financial climate vocational and practical skills are very important in allowing graduates to diversify and become more employable. Twice as many people are failing to find work within two years of graduating than was the case a decade ago, so my view is that if you can get an alternative set of practical skills, as well as combining that with a grounded knowledge of the theory related to that subject, it will help you to stand out.

What advice would you give to a student about to embark on a study of the media, for example at undergraduate level, in terms of the opportunities it is likely to present?

Experience as much as they can. Media degrees can be quite broad initially and students should make the most of this to experience things they might previously have known little about. And make the most of the expertise and equipment available to them, even if it means taking equipment home just to get to grips with how it works.

There's no need to make career decisions within the first year but keep in mind the importance of industry experience. One way of standing out is to get experience off your own back because it shows you have a keen interest. Many universities will have links with production companies that vaguely resemble graduate recruitment programmes. They are very competitive but work experience can only aid an application. If not, the tutors for the course will most certainly have experience of the industry so I would suggest speaking to them about work experience opportunities and how to stand out.

The last thing I would say is to keep an open mind about the future and keep up to date with changes within the industry. Things are rapidly changing, and although skills and experience gained will be invaluable to individuals, this will not necessarily prepare them for walking into a creative role as soon as they leave education.

ESSENTIALS

Edited by Peter Wall
http://www.routledge.com/books/series/ALEVEL/

AS FILM STUDIES
The Essential Introduction
2nd Edition
Sarah Casey Benyahia, Freddie Gaffney and **John White**
2008: 246×174: 414pp • Pb: 978-0-415-45433-9: **£19.99**

A2 FILM STUDIES
The Essential Introduction
2nd Edition
Sarah Casey Benyahia, Freddie Gaffney and **John White**
2009: 246×174: 468pp • Pb: 978-0-415-45436-0: **£19.99**

AS COMMUNICATION AND CULTURE
The Essential Introduction
3rd Edition
Peter Bennett and **Jerry Slater**
2008: 246×174: 340pp • Pb: 978-0-415-45512-1: **£19.99**

A2 COMMUNICATION AND CULTURE
The Essential Introduction
Peter Bennett and **Jerry Slater**
2009: 246×174: 336pp • Pb: 978-0-415-47160-2: **£19.99**

AS MEDIA STUDIES
The Essential Introduction for AQA
3rd Edition
Philip Rayner and **Peter Wall**
2008: 246×174: 360pp • Pb: 978-0-415-44823-9: **£19.99**

A2 MEDIA STUDIES
The Essential Introduction for AQA
2nd Edition
Anthony Bateman, Peter Bennett, Sarah Casey Benyahia, Jacqui Shirley and **Peter Wall**
2010: 246×174: 320pp • Pb: 978-0-415-45735-0: **£19.99**

AS MEDIA STUDIES
The Essential Introduction for WJEC
Anthony Bateman, **Sarah Casey Benyahia**, **Claire Mortimer** and **Peter Wall**
2011: 246×174: 320pp • Pb: 978-0-415-61334-7: **£19.99**

A2 MEDIA STUDIES
The Essential Introduction for WJEC
Anthony Bateman, **Peter Bennett**, **Sarah Casey Benyahia** and **Peter Wall**
2010: 246×174: 352pp • Pb: 978-0-415-58659-7: **£19.99**